Thomas Morris

A House for the Suburbs

Thomas Morris

A House for the Suburbs

Reprint of the original, first published in 1861.

1st Edition 2022 | ISBN: 978-3-37504-179-3

Verlag (Publisher): Salzwasser Verlag GmbH, Zeilweg 44, 60439 Frankfurt, Deutschland
Vertretungsberechtigt (Authorized to represent): E. Roepke, Zeilweg 44, 60439 Frankfurt, Deutschland
Druck (Print): Books on Demand GmbH, In de Tarpen 42, 22848 Norderstedt, Deutschland

A HOUSE

FOR THE SUBURBS;

SOCIALLY AND ARCHITECTURALLY SKETCHED.

BY

THOMAS MORRIS,

MEMBER OF THE ROYAL INSTITUTE OF BRITISH ARCHITECTS.

SECOND EDITION.

LONDON:

SIMPKIN, MARSHALL, & Co.,

STATIONERS' HALL COURT.

MDCCCLXI.

12, REGENT STREET, LONDON.

PREFACE.

WHILE annotators are expected to invest themselves with the sentiments of the authors they elucidate, and painters to delineate from well chosen points of view, the essayist may be equally required to adapt his style to the subject on which he writes: thus, when that " skilfull artist, Master Guillim," had to say that some furs contain more than one colour, he did it in this way, " Furres consisting of more than one colour are either of two colours or more than two," deeming no doubt such deliberation of expression appropriate to the dignity of " heraldrie," and befitting a " Pursuivant at Armes ;" nor have architectural writers been always free from a feeling of like elevation.

[The

The Lawyer in his dry recitals, the
Architect in his specification of materials and
detail, has no latitude for the imagination,—
" a place for everything and everything in its
place" being as imperative with them as with
the Lexicographer himself. " A HOUSE FOR
THE SUBURBS," however, has not appeared
to demand extreme precision, but to admit of
adequate representation by the characterising
lines, articulating dots, and supporting touches
of a sketch, rather than to call for the elabo-
ration of a picture; and it is with this impression I presume to lay my slight pencillings
before the Reader.

SECOND EDITION.

My little piebald, though all too weak for
the shock of the hastilude, brings me a second
time to the quintain of criticism, and secures
for me the grateful privilege of thanking alike

those from whom corrective or complimentary
opinions have been received. Let me hope
that the benefit due to the first will be apparent; but the gratifying encouragement derived
from the other has to be avowed, and I
thankfully avow it. An inadvertence that
provoked a sinister thrust from one hard censor
has been remedied, my surcoat is *regularly*
Marshalled, and now, Sir *Sabre de bois*,
I trustingly attend the call " To achievement."

Carlton Chambers, 12, Regent Street,

1861.

Illustrations.

———◆———

A HOUSE FOR THE SUBURBS.

THANKS to the modern Genius of Speed and the Science of the Rail, a wholesome future is in store for us. I say the modern Genius—as distinguishable from the ancient charioteer, who went too fast for his age, and came to so disastrous a *spill*—while his compeer of the locomotive rejoices in a time whose motto is " Progress ;" from accidents he gathers experience, and starts anew with the elements of future success, on a mission fraught with social changes not dreamt of in our fathers' philosophy.

They will best appreciate the improved intercourse between London and its environs who recollect the *stage coaches* to Paddington, Hammersmith, or Hackney — the stopping

B

and horn-blowing at every turn—the time
consumed on the journey, and the money
charged for it. Our Bankers from Lombard
Street now reach the sea-coast by the time
they used to arrive at Clapham.

Yet it is less to gradual advance and
accumulation of experience than to the dis-
closures of subtle, unseen and mysterious
agencies vouchsafed to recent generations, that
we differ from the civilized nations of a remote
antiquity, who, in intellectual and perceptive
endowments, in poetic impulse and the appre-
ciation of organic beauty, were, and remain, in
many respects, our superiors. Earth, water,
air, and fire, sufficed in the old time ; but
modern analysts after denying to the latter the
power to destroy a single particle of primitive
matter, have ascertained the existence of more
than sixty atomic or irreducible bodies, and
discoveries which to day appear the visions of
philosophy are by to-morrow adopted as

things of practical routine. Gaslighting, for
instance, has lost its charm of wonder,
before the old oil lamps, that served to make
" a darkness visible," are forgotten, or ex-
tinguishers for the links and flambeaux of
running footmen, have disappeared from the
stately portals of western squares. The
decomposition of coal, and the separation of its
illuminating from its heat-bearing constituents
and their application to opposite uses with an
exact economy, have already ceased to create
surprise, though the means of light, conveyed
for miles to streets and habitations, is ready to
spring into brightness by a touch, while the resi-
duum gives power to the engine that surpasses
the race-horse in its speed and urges to swift-
ness the camels of the seas. An inch of water
is converted into a foot of steam, and a mighty
potency evolved from a single pound of coke.

Another agency, not mysterious or unseen,
for its machinery is everywhere in obvious and

busy motion, has by its influence and importance a claim to be ranked among the social subtleties of modern times; and that agency is, the Post-Office.

But wondrous above all are the effects of electricity, which, travelling under pavements, over house-tops, along hedge-rows, and amid the recesses of the deep, removes all trace of time and distance, so that the command of an impatient Oberon—

> " And be thou here again
> " Ere the Leviathan can swim a league,"

may soon be literally obeyed with fact instead of fancy; and the grave manipulator may say, with Shaksperian Puck—

> " I'll put a girdle round about the earth
> " In forty minutes."

The pursuits of the City and vocations of the Town are about to be exercised by a tidal race, whose daily ebb and flow will

be as regular and decided as those of Father
Thames himself. The population of London
is largely sustained by the continuous influx
of provincial recruits, who never lose their
pastoral associations, and though engrossed
for a while with novelty and excitement, return
with the pure affection of an early love to
homes " exempt from public haunts ;" and they
must hail the daily change from worldly care
to Nature's quietude,—the healthful alternation of activity and ease now rendered prac-
ticable,—as a movement of promise for body
and mind for To-day and Hereafter.

The doom of intramural sepulture has
become the signal for extramural life, and the
very altars, from which the holy incense of
praise and prayer has ceased to rise, are
about to follow in this remarkable exodus.

The onward current of events which
brings about the consummation of every

appointed career and gathers to the storehouse
of the past the temple, the oak, and the
patriarch, bears on its surface the Union of
Benefices Act, with its prospective destruction
of City churches; but its operation will be
softened by the absence of popular sympathy
with the buildings it destroys. Erected after
a sort of stereotyped design, cleverly adapted
to particular sites, frequently presenting graceful interiors, though occasionally overcharged
with cumbrous fittings, they are externally as
meagre, bald and ugly as anti-classicists could
well desire.

Based upon London's great, and to those
who did not see the blessing and improvement it foreran, oh how great calamity—that
drove her citizens into the surrounding fields:
fields where many indeed perished, but which
the more affluent never wholly forsook—
erecting rather their houses upon the spots
where their sad unsheltered bivouacs had

taken place; the churches, rising in a prim completeness, and precision of plan, afforded little space for commemorative objects; while from the exigencies of the time or a presumed incompatability with the style and fashion of the day—the decorative arts of a previous age were neglected, and the strong associating link with old important families, possessed by many a timeworn fane, such as that treasury of monumental wealth for instance on the river side at Chelsea, is altogether wanting here.

Court patronage ran then, as now, in deep but very narrow channels, and the number of commissions showered upon Wren were more than enough for a single mind or an individual reputation; but had the designs instead of being hurried into immediate effect, been refined upon, and their elementary conception developed with patient regard to composition; — had the lamp of sacrifice, lighted as it were at the embers of the fire,

and shining with the refulgence due to an
artificial atmosphere, to expend its force in a
convulsion of vivid brightness, then to die,—
burnt with a more constant flame, a clothing
of rich yet chastened ornamentation of which
they are susceptible and worthy, such as the
cathedral and some others are even now
receiving, such indeed as all ecclesiastical
architects have learnt to feel requisite in
whatever style they work, might have been
added by later hands, and these edifices would
have possessed ligaments of veneration so
difficult to break, that their existence would
have been fought for as stoutly as the City
Charter.

It is not in their architectural phase that
these buildings have the strongest ground of
admiration, but in the circumstances under
which they were reared. Out of ninety-seven
churches within the walls only twelve were
left, the inhabitants of the city were over-

whelmed by losses, difficulties, privation, cares
and deep affliction; but prostrated as they
were they displayed a true heroic devotion
that constitutes their works the grandest
memorial of English devotion we possess.
Some testimony is surely due to pious self-
denying labour such as this; and when the
churches yield to secular convenience, to rise
it may be, with renewed usefulness, as folds,
in places to which the flocks have withdrawn
it is not too much to hope that the steeples
and spires may be spared, to raise their taper
heads like minarets on high, and afford their
welcome relief to the general view of England's
capital.

With regard to the fifty new churches for
London, Westminster, and the Suburbs, provided for in the ninth year of Queen Anne,
it was expressly enacted that they should be
of stone or other proper materials, that each
should have a tower or steeple, and that no

interment should be made within or under the sacred edifice, power being given to purchase when necessary and render parochial pieces of land in other places for the purpose of sepulture—a most enlightened and exemplary step, though fraught with the alienation of sentiment mentioned above. The first presentations were reserved to the crown, and the buildings were, as the title of the act shews, not confined to the City of London, one " scite" being indicated near the " Maypole in the Strand," and another at East Greenwich. A sum of four thousand pounds a year was appropriated to the repair of Westminster Abbey, and six thousand a year to the completion of the Hospital and its Chapel at Greenwich.

It is a very neat example of the legerdemain of indirect taxation, which by a slightly extended base of operation and disguising, a church rate in the cloak of a coal tax drew ample funds into the exchequer, while the citizens, more than ever grateful, regarded as the work of public munificence a few churches for themselves, with incumbents not of their own choosing, though they virtually paid for all they obtained, beside providing largely for other places ; but Doctor Smiles had not then revealed the power and example of " SELF-HELP."

With St. Paul's, central in position and glorious alike in form and destination, characterizing at once the grandeur, the religion, and the site of London, there can be little doubt as to where the *milliarium aureum* of this Christian city ought to be enshrined; though such datum points have not been practically much attended to. The gilt column erected by Augustus in the Forum at Rome, simply represented a goal to which the Italian roads tended, while they really measured from the city gates. The Standard in Cornhill was

but another partial mark. Our London Stone
too, which though now reduced to a ruined
block, is a memorable relic marking a thoroughfare of Roman or of British origin, was never,
perhaps, the positive zero of our viatorial
notation. Each route has most likely always
had its peculiar terminus, as Hyde Park
Corner, " famed St. Giles's Pound," or the
yet more famous " spot, where Hicks's Hall
formerly stood."

The great avenues on the North of the
Thames are of remote origin, but except by
boats and the single road-way over London
Bridge, no means existed for entering the
suburbs on the South till the time of George
the Second.

Agreeing with Mr. Craik, that there is as
much perhaps in a bridge to take hold of the
imagination as in any other work (dome,

column, spire, or star-y-pointing pyramid), let us pass these constructions in rapid review, but without becoming emotional from their grandeur, scientific exemplifications, or stirring associations, and regarding them simply as indicators of London's growth and the change in means of locomotion that brought most of them into existence and which they in return have so much facilitated,—a change that has deprived the Thames of royal and noble passengers, and, one after the other, has driven forth its gay emblazoned barges, till the " Lord Mayor" has come to be the hired vessel of water pic-nics—till watermen have given gradual place to Flemish nags, " the pampered jades of Belgia," and the high-bred Cleveland; as boats, and the horse-litter, have done to the sedan, the square-built springless coach, and the amalgamations of strength, taste, and lightness, that now emanate from Long Acre.

Beginning up stream then, where honest Tug plied and sang, at Chelsea Ferry, taking them as they come, or as we come to them, or precisely speaking in the sequence of position, but neglecting Battersea from its unsuggestive mediocity (except to notice its origin some ninety years ago as a retaliation on the watermen who detained Earl Spencer, the Lord of the Manor, while they finished their dinner, a *course* quite consistent with river principles at an earlier day, as reflected by the writings of John Taylor, the Waterman Poet, who, acting on the motto of " Jack's as good as his master," held in very light respect

" Any proud fool who ne'er so proud or wise,
    That does my needful honest trade despise),"

The light ornate Suspension Bridge, with its pleasing effect of airy prettiness, giving access to the new Park from near the opposite College of the Military Veterans, has precedence; and dating so recently as 1857 the approach through Sloane Street is even yet incomplete.

The Brighton Company's Railway Bridge is a worthy competitor for general admiration, being second to none in the skilful adaptation of material and the accomplishment of a grand result by moderate means. It is remarkable for having, like the Britannia Tube over the Menai, a pier in the mid-stream, here necessitated by contiguity to its suspensory neighbour.

The simple business-like example, with a nearly level roadway at Vauxhall, which does so much credit to the integrity and skill of James Walker, dates from 1811.

Labeyle's Bridge at Westminster was the monument of the victory gained by progressing civilization after a contest of ages with the demons of feudal darkness and the fetters of monopoly. The wool-staplers, the ferrymen and other classes met the project with almost insuperable opposition, and so great was the apprehension of violence when the work had been accomplished, that any attempt to destroy it was constituted a capital crime. Having been provided for by the gambling expedient of a lottery, once so common, it was erected between 1738 and 1747, and, after little more than a century, is giving place to Mr. Page's design with seven arches of cycloidal curve, adopted to meet the difficult and opposed conditions of lowness in respect to the great Parliamentary edifice, and of an elevated headway for the navigation. The most favorable point of view for the Westminster Palace is, however, in front of Juxon's Hall, between the Gate-house and the Lollards' Tower, at Lambeth.

Brunel's Foot Bridge, a thing of beauty and almost of yesterday's accomplishment is, as I have elsewhere said, about to be removed, and therefore not " a joy for ever."

It has long appeared to me that the best line from Westminster to Lambeth would be from Nelson's

" Monumental pillar tall and fair "

to the Orphan Asylum, with a road on the South of Northumberland House, continued by a bridge crossing the river obliquely, a plan no longer likely to shock the public or puzzle the engineer.

Canova the sculptor pronounced Rennie's Waterloo Bridge to be worth a visit from the remotest corner of the earth; and, in 1817, he could hardly have been charged with hyperbole.

Some respect is due to the next in succession, for in Blackfriars we meet the Pontine

c

father of the Thames, designed by Mylne, an
architect of celebrity, and completed in 1771.
It was built by a company having a privilege
to exact a toll for nineteen years.

In Southwark Bridge we have another and
a noble example by Rennie, completed in 1819.
It is the shortest of its class, but the enormous
spans of its iron arches give it a magnificence
and simplicity which reflect the greatest credit
on the designer; and the production of the
gigantic castings added to the renown Mr.
Walker, of Rotheram, had already obtained in
connection with an implement of humble but
extensive use, the Flat-iron.

The prosecution of his London works and
such others as Ramsgate Harbour, Plymouth
Breakwater, and the Bell Rock Lighthouse,
was a fitting preliminary to Rennie's master
effort in London Bridge, perhaps the latest
grand example of the true masonic, homo-

geneous and monumental style of building
by which the Thames will ever be spanned.
Yet was the stability of this majestic work
jeopardised by an oversight in removing instead
of cutting off the piles employed in the
temporary means of its erection.

Even more singular in its nature, more
difficult of execution, and calling forth energy
and perseverance in an unexampled degree, is
that monument of Sir Marc Isambard Brunel,
—the Thames Tunnel.

Within little more than a century then
some eight millions sterling have been spent
in facilitating access with the suburbs of the
South, and the Metropolitan Board of Works
appear very properly alive to the necessity
of removing the tolls from some or all
of these, which have now come to be as
obnoxious as were those of the highways
a few years ago. This step is certainly

most desirable for the relief of the over-crowded thoroughfares and general public convenience.

The highest engineering skill having meanwhile been turned to the highways, not of the Metropolis alone, but throughout the country, England attracted with regard to them, the admiration of the world. But the wonders of the Road are forgotten in the triumphs of the Rail; the *chef d'œuvres* of Telford and McAdam must now give place to the iron lines of Stephenson and Brunel; and these, by means of bridges, embankments, and tunnels, are being rapidly extended into the very municipal heart, commercial centre, and seat of traffic.

In the few months even since these lines were first written, the important Victoria station at Pimlico has been opened: The railway substitute for Hungerford bridge, by

which its suspending chains will be relieved
from their original duty to serve a similar
purpose at Clifton, has been commenced and a
practical assurance thus given that ere long
Hungerford market will be transformed into
the busy terminus of Charing Cross.

The Metropolitan railway has in the mean
time been silently burrowing between Paddington, and Farringdon Street, removing by
its progress the shadowy character, once at-
taching to the plan of a grand focal turntable
and bringing to the verge of accomplishment,
the object so long advocated by Mr. Charles
Pearson. The *rail* Penumbra now is Mr. Train.

If the Royal Exchange and Trafalgar
Square be taken as *foci*, we may reach
a radial distance of ten miles from either
with ease in an hour, without resorting
to the concentrated energy of the Brighton
or Western expresses, and allowing for a

mile's walk at each end of the line; so that an area of nearly a quarter of a million of acres is rendered very accessible, and points locally distant are brought into close proximity, with regard to that great arcanum of human effort—TIME.

Whether those engaged in the lower and more laborious occupations may soon enjoy the advantage of village homes is uncertain; but the Railway system of the Metropolis is as yet so infantile and transitional, that the results of the next twenty years may exceed all present expectation. That such a relief is available to, and extensively adopted by every superior grade, becomes manifest to the spectator on London Bridge, at nine in the morning, or the later hours of the afternoon.

The counties of Middlesex, Essex, Kent, and Surrey,—to say nothing of Lamb's " hearty, homely, loving Hertfordshire," (which stretches its promontories into the circuit,) with their varieties of surface geological feature, scenery, and climate,—offer respective inducements to those who seek to fix their firesides beyond the incessant din of busy streets, where the mind may throw off its daily harness, and the bodily garb of "formal cut" give place to the jacket and the *wide-awake;* for, as Sterne has it, "a man's body and his mind are exactly like a jerkin and a jerkin's lining—rumple the one and you rumple the other." We cannot relieve the one without benefit to the other; and where may we so confidingly look for this relief as to the sweet and cunning hand of Nature?

> " Expatiate in our proud suburban shades,
>   Of branching elm, that never sun pervades."

As a practical illustration of the solace to be thus derived, let us listen to the concluding words of Repton's well-known work:—" The most valuable lesson now left me to communicate," he says, " is this. I am convinced that the delight I have always taken in landscapes and gardens, without any reference to their quantity or appropriation, or without caring whether they are forests or rosaries, or whether they were palaces, villas, or cottages, while I had leave to admire their beauties, and even to direct their improvement, have been the chief source of that large portion of happiness which I have enjoyed through life." And he lays down his pen to echo the cry—

" Allons, mes amis, il faut cultiver nos Jardins."

But while Content rules the garden, the temple of her rosy sister, Health, is seated *more poetarum*, amid the neighbouring green swards and brown heaths, where fragrant thyme receives the golden light, and sweet-breath'd violets more deeply tinge the purple shade.

Then, again, the children nursed in the rough cradle of old Sylvanus are, *certes*, children of a larger growth, and they multiply also in an extraordinary numerical ratio,—for, whatever may be the statement of the Registrar-General, I believe the predominance of large families in the country, as compared with Town, is very marked indeed, though the result may be jointly due to births and to migration.

Out of the area involved in our boundary must be deducted, not only the busy nucleus, but several tracts which are low, marshy, or otherwise unsuited to residential purposes. For such objects the slopes and elevated tables are chiefly in request, commanding as they necessarily do, the advantages of dryness, prospect, and ventilation. If there be, further, a permeable soil, good water, easy access, cheerful aspect, and a neighbourhood free from objectionable circumstances, such a fulfilment of all reasonable requirements imparts the highest relative value. But land of this character is generally doomed to rapid and minute subdivision.

The existing arrangements for supplying water to London and its environs suffer by comparison with those of Rome two thousand years ago. The population of the great Imperial city with its suburbs, according to the most reliable sources, was only about 700,000; yet in what luxurious profusion did its high-arched aqueducts lave its hill-tops and pour into every quarter the liquid element of health, cleanliness, and pleasure. Forty millions of cubic feet or six times that number of gallons flowed daily through the conduits, supplying the personal and domestic wants, private and public baths, and the theatrical seas of the Naumachiae.

The collective result of ten London companies may be taken at eighty millions of gallons daily; and the quantity abstracted by breweries and distilleries, dye and bleaching works, mills and manufactories, railways and nursery grounds, for flushing the sewers, for watering roads, extinguishing fires, and other " distractions," would probably equal the amount used for the sea fights of the Coliseum and similar demands of the ancient Capital. While the individual supply for the Roman, therefore, of the first Christian ages was upwards of three hundred and forty gallons, the Londoner of the present day receives but thirty.

The superiority of London's local resources may have precluded the expensive means resorted to by Rome and her provincial cities; but the unwelcome surmise still obtrudes itself that nice personal habits formed no very distinguishing trait of our ancestral citizens, and many a scourging epidemic has no doubt

been due to indifference and perversity on
this great sanatory point. So lately even
as 1834, the " intake " of one company
was in " close proximity " to the outlet
of the Ranelagh sewer! *A dead take in*
I should presume to observe to the poor
consumers, and it may be noticed that the
arrangements for pouring filth into the
Thames, above the new source of supply
at Hampton, more than keep pace at this
very time with the means for preventing
contamination.

One fourth of the quantity supplied to the
Metropolis is furnished by the New River, yet
how much more of ridicule than gratitude
attended the devotion of Sir Hugh Middleton,
to whose memory, in these days, a fountain of
crystal purity would be but an appropriate
though tardy memorial. The New River is
almost the only instance of an aqueduct we
have; and being formed on the simplest plan,

without arches or imposing constructions, is so far distinct from the Italian examples, a fact which may be noticed as favorable to the asserted existence of aqueducts among the Greeks, although the principle of the arch was unknown to them.

Sir Hugh commenced his work in 1608, but it is worthy of remark, that twenty-six years earlier Peter Morris had, by the introduction of a tidal engine, or "artificial forcier," at London Bridge (powerful enough we are told to throw a stream over the church of St. Magnus), laid the foundation of that system upon which so many consecutive discoveries having been engrafted, such as the effect of atmospheric pressure, the application of steam and concomitant improvement in hydraulic apparatus give it the highly developed character it now displays ; embodying in its statistics some eight millions of money, steam power equal to more than seven thousand horses, and above two thousand miles of main-pipes and branches.

Should these remarks suggest to limping wits a somewhat popular form of monument as befitting the services of stout old Peter, let me remind them of the plan of Pekin. The entrance to that city lies between two temples, one to heaven and the other to the inventor of agriculture. The Chinese are evidently grateful to the hand that feeds them and Londoners may well be thankful to the innovator of Pumps.

To the Legislature we owe the greatly improved condition of the water furnished, and the boon of a constant supply is foreshadowed by recent enactments. The great social importance of the subject must recommend it indeed to the care of every considerate government; nor will it suffice to deal with general results alone, it is necessary that there should be an abundant supply to every house, and under the very hand and free control of every occupant; but this desirable state of things can hardly be effected, while some companies are permitted to charge three times as much as others.

Of the large district subject to the Local Management Acts, a very great proportion has not yet come under the practical influence of the Main Drainage system, which is, no doubt, destined to effect benefits of a very important kind; although, as concerns the purification of the river, and the improvement of the contiguous property, no plan can be successful which does not provide for the exclusion from the stream of the bilgewater and excretia of the docks and manufactories below bridge. It is only thus the capabilities of the river as a liquid road—a silent highway—can be adequately laid open.

Among the points of superiority possessed by Rome over every other city of antiquity, few were more valuable than the drains or cloacæ, nor in the same utilitarian range has any modern capital proved a rival to our own; but great as she has long been in this respect, it was reserved for the present generation to conceive the comprehensive system, and to execute the truly wonderful and unexampled project, destined perhaps to furnish distant futurity with the most unique of all memorials of London's greatness. We must not, however, allow the attractions of high level, low level, and outfall sewers; of tunnels, shafts, and overflows; of pumping stations and hydraulic powers; of men employed by thousands, and bricks consumed by millions, to arrest attention, but looking with pleasing hope to a speedy and commensurate success, for those engaged in this battle with Mephitis pursue the even tenor of our way.

In undrained districts it is generally inexpedient to adopt a sunk or basement story; otherwise accommodation may be thus obtained in a very economical manner, especially in small houses built in pairs, by which mode the disproportionate height of a single house is obviated.

This has lately been stigmatized as " Cockney fashion ; " but let me in all courtesy suggest that there is no ground for sarcasm ;—nothing is *Cockney* that does not violate fitness and simplicity. The different conditions of life, apart from relative status, render widely different things appropriate and convenient. " A cottage with a double coach-house" was an obvious incongruity, and fairly became the sport of the satirist. But for one of more vaulting ambition, there are many " humble livers in content," who, though fond of pure air, gladly leave predial reforms to the able hands

D

of Mr. Mechi; spade and fork husbandry to
the championship of Miss Martineau; and the
poultry-yard to another "blue," with all its
interesting details of gallinaceous physiology.
Though such indifference may disappoint
the *soft-egg* theorist of a weekly review, who
deserves to be pecked by some crowing hen of
the poultry press for hatching an addlepated
misconception.

Middlesex stands in somewhat the same
relation to the four metropolitan counties
that Europe does to the other quarters of the
globe. Though of inferior size, it is the great
seat of civilization, intellect, and enterprise,
therefore it will have our first consideration
in a rapid glance at the features of each
with a view to the choice of sites.

The surface presents much variety, and
though there are extensive flats near the
Thames, its altitudes at Highgate, Hamp-

stead, and Harrow, surpass all others near London; but a sort of physical compensation seems to exist, for in the lower parts there is the light friable loam of which the celebrated bricks made in the Cowley districts near Uxbridge consist; while the higher lands are often clayey and unfertile, though this latter is of secondary importance where abundance of manure can be so readily obtained.

The air is mild, and a supply of soft wholesome water is afforded by the numerous rivulets. Several railways pass over the district and give improved access to many additional points; but otherwise its most eligible localities had in a long course of time become thoroughly appropriated, subdivided, and *used up*. And so with Milton

" To-morrow to fresh fields and pastures new."

We will now step into Essex, indeed a

very land of pastures, though not of that
elevated, dry, and upland character most
suited to our object. Anciently the tides
passed over it so extensively as to allow our
Danish enemies to follow the bed of the Lea
up to Ware; and as one of the many instances
in which Bellona becomes the handmaid of
science, the tactics of Alfred led to the recla-
mation of a large and fertile tract nearly on
a dead level as regards the general area,
though with some occasional undulations,
dotted in the olden time with monastic
houses, and now with hamlets, forests, and
parks, but it is essentially maritime, and
chiefly remarkable for its docks, canals, and
works of a marine character.

It is traversed by the Eastern Counties
and Blackwall systems of Railways, but the
most eligible portion abuts upon the western
boundary, where the " sedgy Lea," a favourite
resort of the " brothers of the angle ;" the

Northern and Eastern Railway, and the Old
Cambridge Road, run in close and parallel
proximity.

Redolent of tanyards, dank with cress-
pits and yellow vegetation, its people densely
crowded among huge sheds and factories, the
first features of suburban Kent are most
unpromising to the pictorial eye; but how
soon do the London Bridge Lines transport
us to the heights of the Royal Observatory,
Shooter's Hill, and (the favored of art and
nature) Sydenham. While the Chatham and
Dover line, embracing London with extended
arms, is calculated yet further to facilitate suburban transit, but trains at short intervals would
be a worthy exchange for monster cargoes.

The Kentish atmosphere is supposed to
be affected in some degree by vapours from
the sea and river, and to be less equable than
that of some other places. There may be

less diluvial soil overlying the rock, whether
of ironstone, chalk, or rag, and circumspection may be necessary, but the scenery and
arboreous luxuriance is nowhere surpassed,
while the great facility of transit afforded, by
the positive network of iron roads, is alone
sufficient to bring it into especial request.

A few remarks on the remaining county,
Surrey, will complete this brief survey. The
immediate bank of the Thames on which
stand Lambeth, Vauxhall, Battersea, &c. is
equally low with that on the Middlesex side,
but at a short remove from the river we have
the fine gravelly elevation extending from
Clapham Common westward, here and there
abraded and falling into loam, clay, or chalk,
but singularly happy in superficial contour, in
alternation of hill and dale, in great diversity
of scenery and extent of view.

It has long enjoyed high repute for its

healthy climate. " For the soil," saith Speed,
"it is better stored for game than grain, and
the wholesomeness of the air issues from the
sandiness of the soil, notwithstanding which
it is wealthy enough both in corn and pasture, especially in the North parts, towards
the River of Thames."

Besides the " Royal-tower'd Thame," it is
watered by the Wandle and the curious Mole,
so called from its long-supposed property of
flowing under ground for a couple of miles,
between Leatherhead and Dorking, but this
attribute is now classed with " vulgar errors."

The railway service is performed by the
London and South Western Company's lines
to Southampton, Windsor, &c., and these are
connected with the London Bridge series by
several branches, rendering the communication very complete with Pimlico, Charing
Cross, and the City.

From its fine open upland character, and local proximity to the quarter of the Court and Fashion, Surrey may be said to contain the Belgravian suburb, and its map is thickly studded with coronets, imparting to its best districts a *ton*, which leads, in some instances, to very high or *fancy* prices.

Some years ago the Commissioners of Sewers presented to me a copy of their map of London and its environs, indicating not only the position of places, but giving, in figures, their altitudes above a certain datum; and I have found this a most valuable addition to the ordinary map. It may, I believe, be had of Mr. Wyld, at Charing Cross, and those who are seeking residential property would do well to consult it, though they must by no means be wholly governed by it, as there are many circumstances to be considered*.

* If this valuable map be proprietary or out of print, it leaves a desideratum in geodesy.

Bacon thought a man might as well build himself a prison as a house upon an ill-chosen site, and he cautions us not merely to avoid unwholesome, but unequal air. " In some places," he says, " the wind gathereth as in troughs, so you shall have, and that suddenly, as great diversity of heat and cold, as if you dwelt in several places. Neither is it ill air only that maketh an ill seat, but ill ways, ill markets ; and, if you consult with Momus, ill neighbours." It is difficult to ensure amiability, but they who are the least censorious have the best chance of being pleased in this respect, and those who exercise the truest judgment in the selection of their own homes are most likely to be followed by the intelligent.

Nothing can be more conducive to the architect's success than a well-chosen position for his work, and no part of his duty more urgently demands his careful study ; though it not unfrequently happens that all choice on the subject is precluded, by some step taken under the erroneous impression that nothing but the building would have any interest for him, and in utter unconsciousness of the artistic advantages pertaining to one spot over another.

Some easy people too are apt to console themselves on such matters with the remark, that it all depends on taste, as though taste were very chance, according to the old dogma, " De gustibus non est disputandum." But in these times we come to a different conclusion, and regard taste as demonstrable, in presence and degree, by the positive or negative indications of an infallible, though mental, scale.

In coming to speak of the choice of situation, it is not my. purpose to notice the practices of certain parasites, who farm

the assistance of unfledged tyros, and defraud
their employers of the services of experienced
and responsible professors; but the office
of selection has been so directly arrogated
by landscape gardeners, who seem bent upon
leaving their own province for the structural
arena, that it is almost a matter of necessity
to admit their claims or to refute them.

Richard Morris is of opinion that, previous
to the erection of a dwelling, " it is most proper
to consult the architect as to the form and
plan of the proposed house, and especially as
to the *materials;* and at all times it would
be advantageous to the proprietor, and satisfactory to the architect, if the landscape
gardener were consulted upon the most
appropriate situation;" but he forgot that he
who has a soul for materials alone is not
an architect, any more than one is fit to be
deemed a physician, who stands in need of
correction from the apothecary.

Humphrey Repton admits that it is impossible to describe the situation applicable to a house, without at the same time describing the sort of house applicable to the situation; yet, with this conviction in his mind, he would determine the spot for a dwelling, and then leave the architect, who was never shewn the place he had to deal with, to work out his plans blindfold. He relates with perfect nonchalance a case of this sort, where the consequences of such meddling were most detrimental to his patron's interest; but he of course threw all the blame upon the erring follower of Ictinus, and, with his accustomed self-complacency, adds, "I have therefore long been compelled to make architecture a *branch* of my profession."

This unfortunate exigence, (till his eldest son came to the rescue,) involved him in continual and—but I write with a charitable pen, which splutters at the record—not altogether unmerited difficulties. The son however rose to an architectural distinction that shews he did not regard the art as a mere branch of landscape gardening, and no doubt felt quite able to fix the position of buildings for himself.

Who but the architect indeed can rightly conceive, not only the economic demands, but the scenic effects of and from the house—its terraces and accessories, with their mutual adaptations and relative advantages—forming in his mind a vivid picture of the consummated whole?

In the treatment of

" Hill, dale, and shady woods, and sunny plains,
　And liquid lapse of running streams,"

an artistic sentiment is demanded similar to that which guides the painter in the highest class of landscape composition. The winding lake, with its sinuous boundary; the level glade,

" Where peaceful rivers, soft and slow,
　Amid the verdant landscape flow;"

the gentle rise, with lines of long but varied
sweep; the sharper knoll; the unexpected
vista; the abrupt eminence, with crisp arti-
culations of abraded rock; and catching lights,
contrasted with the deepened shadow of some
near ravine, are open to the eclectic pencil
now as they were to Claude and to Salvator
Rosa. To display the painter's feeling by
earthworks, roads, water, and constructions;
to give to the practical cartoon its " mould of
form," constitute the scope and purpose of
landscape gardening. Artists of various race
may possess the power of doing what is indicated here; but when it has to be done in
connection with a building, the edifice must
form the jewel, of which the scenery is the
setting—the portrait, to which it is the
drapery, and must be entirely subservient.
It is no wonder, therefore, that the progress
of landscape gardening has been mainly due
to architects; and the choice of situation
should unquestionably be left to them, until

we have a fitting dictator to a Le Nôtre, a
Kent, a Chambers, or a Nash, names well
represented by the Burtons, Smirkes, and
Pennethornes of the present day.

The feudal barons, regarding security as
the chief object, erected their castles in the
most elevated, and often almost inaccessible
positions; while the religious communities,
courting fertility, and assured of peace,
or at least hoping for it, selected the bosom
of the rich, well watered vale;—but gleaning
experience from each of these, we may also
indulge considerations with which they were
wholly unacquainted.

We abandon the summit to obtain shelter
from the bleakness of its unsubdued and cutting
winds, inimical alike to animal and vegetable
life, and therefore depriving such a position of
those appropriate and ornamental accompani-
ments which are so essential to a perfect house.

The depression of the valley must also be avoided, on account of dampness, stagnant air, want of prospect, and because a house is never seen more disadvantageously than when looked down upon.

An elevated " knap, " or slope, high enough to command the distant prospect, yet not too high for easy approach, backed by a curtain of woodland, and covered with graceful foliage, will afford the greatest combination of natural advantages; and a house so seated will form an agreeable object, when viewed from a distance, as it neither falls below the horizon nor rudely breaks the sky.

" But this is up-hill work," the reader may exclaim : " I am led to the top, then to the bottom, and thus far up again, yet there is no house within eyeshot. What would " All round the Wrekin" be to this ? does my

architectural guide propose to train me for
' A Londoner's Walk to the Land's End?' or
think me as nimble as a Llangollen goat, and
as fond of the *Alpenstock* as they who spend
a week at the Righi, or ramble ' on foot
through Tyrol,' and his grandiloquence savors
of a hundred acres at the least?"

True; but let me hope the labour has not
been altogether fruitless; and, if there be but
little satisfaction, some advantage may arise
from having seen the places to be avoided,
as well as those to be chosen. You have at
length reached a spot where the bounteous
hand of Nature has done much to help the
business of Art. The price will be high, but
you are unrestricted as to quantity; and it
would be easy to adduce many instances in
which all essential properties are attained on
a very moderate space: we will therefore discourse, in returning, on the value and capacity
of a single acre of land.

E

There is a sort of floating traditional impression, that some precious particle of earth in the heart of the City has brought after the rate of a million an acre; but how far the love of *round* numbers and poetic licence are here involved I do not pretend to decide, but a hundred thousand pounds would, in many cases, represent the marketable value of the fee simple of that quantity*.

An enormous realization is therefore open to the Bank of England, whenever it may think fit to consolidate its straggling offices into a grand convenient edifice, and appropriate the superfluous part of the site to a new Stock Exchange and other monetary establishments, with a dividing thoroughfare from Threadneedle Street to Lothbury.

* At a sale of a portion of the site of the old Rainbow Tavern, adjoining the Union Bank, Fleet Street, on Saturday, the 14th instant, the price realised was at the enormous rate of £.900,000 per acre.—*Builder*, January 21, 1860.

Such prices are mainly dependent on the character of the frontage, and proximity to some important centre, whether in the depths of Thames Street or on the higher regions of the Bank and Paternoster Row.

The average value of land in the four home counties does not seem to exceed fifty pounds per acre; but the benefits of rapid conveyance for produce, and improving agricultural intelligence, are likely to become an admirable succedaneum for exploded regulations, which were far more hurtful in their restriction than beneficial in a protective sense.

Facilitated passenger traffic in the vicinity of London has a certain equalizing tendency on residential property; but it acts rather by improving the distant than by depressing the near; and a well-circumstanced acre, though ten miles from Town, will occasionally produce its thousand pounds.

The annexed Table is presumed to afford an approximate view of the value of first-class building land under ordinary circumstances; but the question is subject to so many influences, that it is put forward with extreme diffidence, and I court correction. A plan lies before me as I write, on which plots within a few yards of each other differ as 1 and 2, chiefly on account of their respective levels.

TABLE
OF THE
APPROXIMATE VALUE, PER ACRE,
OF
BUILDING LAND NEAR LONDON.

		£.
At 7 miles distant	. .	500
,, 8 ,, ,,	. .	430
,, 9 ,, ,,	. .	370
,, 10 ,, ,,	. .	320
,, 11 ,, ,,	. .	280
,, 12 ,, ,,	. .	250

Let us now turn to the question of space, and familiarize the mind with some simple form of computation. A sort of royal road to land-measure, easily trodden by those who disdain the stricter path of poles and chains.

An acre, for instance, contains 4,840 superficial yards; and, if we would reduce this to a square shape, it appears that seventy yards is the nearest length for the side, though somewhat too large, as 70 multiplied by itself gives 4,900, instead of 4,840; but, with this caution, it will be very convenient for our purpose.

Again, seventy yards are equal to two hundred and ten feet, of which, if we take the half, or one hundred and five feet, it will represent the side of a square containing a quarter of an acre; thus:—

APPROXIMATE DIMENSIONS OF A SQUARE
ACRE IN FEET.

210 Feet.

ONE QUARTER OF AN ACRE. 105 Feet.	ONE QUARTER OF AN ACRE. 105 Feet.
ONE QUARTER OF AN ACRE.	ONE QUARTER OF AN ACRE.

210 Feet.

This very simple diagram will afford a ready means of judging the contents of plots of various shapes, and the only correction is an abatement of 1-80th, or at the rate of three pence in the pound sterling.

Houses of medium size in London, though of considerable pretension externally,—such as those in Regent Street, for example,—occupy less on an average than the twentieth part of an acre. Semi-detached houses near the Metropolis, of the yearly value of a hundred pounds, have seldom more than a quarter of an acre allotted to each; and the engraved block plan of a house near Wimbledon Park, Surrey, is put forward to shew the scope afforded by a site of a hundred feet wide by two hundred and twenty in depth, and containing therefore twenty-two thousand superficial feet, or just about half an acre.

I invite attention to these statements the more earnestly, from a conviction that many people, proposing to reside in the suburbs, demand an extent of land very much greater than their actual objects necessitate; and, when they come to count the cost, think there must be some league to keep up the price. They may thus be able to define their wants more exactly, and will do well to bear in mind that the occupation of un-necessary land is a positive evil, entailing endless expenditure, and inducing sloven-liness. Tillage is out of place; feeding stock a costly affectation; and all idea of commercial farming *infra dig.* in an establish-ment whose every operation should be strictly confined to home use; and the neatness and well-being of every adjunct should testify the owner's easy position and liberal tastes, so that lawns, parterres, shrubberies, bosquets, kitchen gardens, orchards, and pastures, ought to constitute the chief items of the *terrier*.

It is pleasantly shewn, in " Our Farm of
Four Acres and the Money we made by it,"
that economy may be exercised in suburban
homes as well as elsewhere; and I hold the
ladies of that model family beyond all praise
for doing battle with difficulties, and rising,
as they deserved to do, " o'er all the ills of
life victorious."

It is with no disrespect, therefore, and in
no forgetfulness of worldly mutations, that I
contemplate for the fair occupants of my
" house for the suburbs" a perfect immunity
from act or part in the business of the place,
(beyond the high duty of supervision,) and a
spirit above the tart manner and petty huck-
stering habit of which I shall take leave to
extract a note from the work in question:—

" A friend of the writer's, a lady of large
fortune, and mistress of a very handsome
establishment, said, when speaking of her

dairy, 'My neighbourhood has the character
of making very bad butter; mine is invariably
good; and I always get a penny a pound more
for it at the "shop" than my neighbours. If
I have occasion to change the dairymaid, and
the new one sends me up bad butter, I tell
her of it. If it occurs the second time, I
make no more complaints; I go down the
next butter-day, and make it entirely myself,
having her at my side the whole time. I
never find I have to complain again. She
sees how it is made, and she is compelled
to own it is good. I believe that a servant
who is worth keeping will follow any directions, and take any amount of trouble, rather
than see "missus" a second time enter the
kitchen or dairy, to do her work.' Perhaps
the allusion this lady made to the "shop,"
may puzzle the London reader; but in
country places, where more butter is made
in a gentleman's family than is required for
the consumption of the household, it is sent

to—what is frequently—the "shop" of the place, and sold for a penny per pound less than the price for which it is retailed by the shopkeeper. The value of the butter is set off against tea, sugar, cheese, and various other articles required in the family in which the butter is made."

Good housewifery is undoubtedly commendable in every stage, from the palace to the cottage; but what is appropriate to the one, may be wholly out of place in the other;—so that which was praiseworthy in the ladies of the " Farm," with a *large family* to cater for, and money rather " tight," as the phrase upon 'Change is, appears altogether *malapropos* to one of *large fortune*, and mistress of a very " handsome establishment."

Upon ladies of this class a duty of the highest social importance devolves—namely, to form and give a valuable character to the society of the place in which they reside. It attaches to them individually, and constitutes, in my humble belief, one of the great features of Woman's Mission.

I use the term in no affected sense, but simply to express the performance of those rational duties, and the exercise of those better influences, which are so completely within her province and her power; and it is not perhaps an entirely chimerical idea, that there has never been in the whole range of human history a concurrence of circumstances, physical and political, more favourable to the development of female power, in its true and unchallenged sphere, than exist in our own day, and in and about our own Metropolis.

It is a condition of things, due to the natural energies of our race, to strength of purpose, and patience of labour in the mass, guided by the mental vigour with which our reasoning compatriots are endowed—to happy international legislation, and that fortunate domestic system which combines entire subjection with perfect freedom—a system, under which the encouragement of art, the fostering of science, the promotion of commerce, and the countenance of industry keep pace with the widening distinction of purpose, to which men and machinery are respectively applied. The latter being now, though tardily, recognised as the beneficent means of great amelioration to thousands, thus released from heavy and debasing toil, for the prosecution of more fitting avocations, Machinery may be called the labourers' servant, the servants' slave; and he who would oppose its judicious introduction, may be likened to a master who would have no groom, or a mistress who would dispense with housemaids. While machinery, therefore, is daily put to novel uses, the character and value of human labour is improved, and the conditions of our being raised and ameliorated. Though very much, therefore, may remain to be raised and softened, they ought, indeed, to be happy who live in such a case; and they will be happy, if they only feel the blessings they enjoy, and build in their hearts a temple to the Giver of them all.

In the country a sense of this comes most forcibly upon the mind—the wonders of the inorganic world are there most earnestly contemplated, their lessons most deeply written on the heart. As the eye stretches into the vast empyrean, an all-powerful Ruler is proclaimed. Innumerable orbs, refulgent but unconscious, perform in silence their allotted parts; but the gazer feels an inward light " above the brightness of the sun," which stamps him with greater honour than them all. His race alone is admitted to communion with the Omniscient, and can say,—

" O Spirit, that dost prefer,
    Before all Temples, the upright heart and pure,
    Instruct me."

But let such thoughts be ever tempered with humbleness; for who possesses that pure and upright heart, or is free to neglect the ministrations of an earthly temple, or fail

" To love the high embowed roof
    With antique pillars massy proof ? "

It is no common period when the highest in rank pride themselves more on their absolute usefulness than on barren titles;— when they come among us to set an example of freedom from pride; discourse on " common things;" go home full of joy when their labours are appreciated; and are more elated with some expression of humble gratitude than with golden spurs and knightly decorations! If ladies will be also in the van of civilization, let them form a brigade of *Victorian Invincibles:* Moral influence on

their pennon, Home for head-quarters,—
and a campaign will open to them worthier
and greater than any yet recorded by the
pen of grateful Fame. But of this anon.

In a Southern suburb, of the old school,
consideration and respect are said to be based
on a strict accordance with the assumed condition of the banker's book; courtesy is looked
upon as merchandise, and meted out with mer-
cenary exactitude; the equestrian exchanges
no bow with his pedestrian neighbour,—his
joys, hopes, and fears, his health and life,
are subject to one absorbing principle. The
physician consults the symptoms; and Death
or Basinghall Street reveals the deficits of the
banker's book:—

> Thus Satan loads his dice with pelf,
> And wins the wretch concentrated in self.

Much happier, however, were the conditions
under which I had the good fortune to live
for several years previous to my colleagues'

retirement, and my consequent accession to the *reins of office.*

In the City, indeed, a man may candidly inquire, " And who is my neighbour ?"—but here the term had a real and positive signification: its obligations were felt and admitted; a sense of mutual relation and dependence existed; while those little kindnesses passed current that give such agreeable evidence of the good feeling to which we may be indebted, and have our affections awakened by, in a thousand instances, against one opportunity for affording or receiving any more substantial benefit.

> " Life's charities, like light,
>   Spread smilingly afar ;
> But stars approached become more bright,
>   And home is life's own star."

A number of families had recently located themselves on a certain spot, and, taking a gregarious turn, set about the organization

F

of a social system, which was found to work most admirably; and, as it may be applicable to other places, I may be pardoned for attempting, however inadequately, to describe it.

The "Book Club" gave to Paterfamilias one agreeable night each month, and afforded literary pabulum for all the leisure hours during the rest of it. The little republic, scarcely exceeding a dozen in number, comprised our Oxford Vicar,—a Professor of King's, the Principal of the Proprietary School, and a Member of the Bar,—all of Cambridge; a brace of M.D.'s; some who gave their "seven hours to law;" but the Arts were left to my most insufficient representation. With several of these, not only learning, but teaching, may be termed a business, and literature a favourite pursuit;— but the salt of our *noctes bibliothecanæ* were the dear old Boys from *Capel Court*, who were ever ready to intersperse the sober shade of passing facts with sparks of heliotropic brightness. Some were engaged in commerce : most made their daily visit to Town, but others were local magnates.

We had no over-formal, no "buttoned-up" men, who, under the affectation of importance and gravity, exclude themselves from the fellowship for which they feel unfitted, and shrink with fear. Let such, remembering that we are more commonly made ridiculous by affectation than vice, be cowards no longer ; but, uniting courage with humility, submit themselves to the estimate of their fellows,—open their houses, and expand their hearts ; and so, being given to hospitality, fulfil at least one divine injunction.

> " Mild heaven disapproves," as Milton felt,
>> " the care, though wise in show,
>> That with superfluous burden loads the day,
>> And when God sends a cheerful hour, refrains."

We were peripatetic, and moved the
scene from house to house. We arrived
with punctuality, and coffee was served at
eight o'clock. After imbibing that not
inebriating beverage, and exchanging its
concomitant little courtesies, the host for
the evening was called to the chair, supported on either hand by the treasurer and
the secretary. The business then began, in
the correct and formal manner, by a perusal
of the minutes; and, although it may be
thought that the record must necessarily
have been of a most simple kind, the dis-
cussion was just as animated as though it
had taken place in a larger assembly. The
cornucopia of Literature was then emptied
on the table, and a bouquet selected for the
coming month. The works of theologians
were freely admitted, but theological subjects
—·never. General topics after this, with a
libation, as modest in quantity as though we
had been Epizephrii, but of rare and curious

age and quality, usually detained us till the eleventh hour.

A two-guinea subscription covered the purchase and circulation of books, and the fund was augmented by the produce of the last year's works, which were sold to the members, after dinner, at our anniversary meeting—a primitive way of doing the business, but it was our only festival, and if not quite so efficacious as a fancy sale, a volume has at least been known to bring more than its first cost! Can you view without remorse, ye Smiths and Mudies, the innovations you are working in the clubs?

While a member of that little republic, I noticed that, although the books sold for half their average cost, and the current subscription was annually augmented in this ratio, it never doubled itself. According to this view, a subscription of twenty pounds, augmented by ten for old books, would make thirty pounds at the commencement of the second year: half thirty, added to twenty, would be thirty-five for the third year, and so on; but when, let me ask the mathematician, would it arrive at forty pounds? The property of that singular curve, which always approaches a given point but never reaches it, seems here brought into practical application.

Dinners (I do not mean those specious affairs where as many covert purposes lie beneath the tablecloth as there are covers above it, but kindly, cordial, bright, sociable, familiar dinners) do not seem to be easily reducible to club law. We have accomplished " diners"—men, *spirituel* and entertaining, without too much conceit; ladies, who can be lively and unconstrained, yet self-possessed —people who can perform their parts gracefully, treating ceremony like rules of art— to be always acted upon, yet never perceived.

But there is no overcoming an excessive desire to offer something costly, and vouchsafe a welcome by material profusion. We dine " not wisely, but too well." A dinner presents the highest phase of hospitality, and involves skill, ceremony, and expense, beyond all others; nor does the present elegant mode, with so small a display of that which is eatable, and so much of that which is not, greatly simplify the matter. The party are the host's most honoured friends; it is among them he is emulous to shine; and the guests are commensurately on the *qui vive*. No ordinary compliment or token of respect, indeed, surpasses the invitation to dinner, or affords more enjoyment, when the arrangements evince a thorough *savoir faire*; and the facility with which every movement is performed, shews dining to be habitual. Let there, further, be a successful cast of the *dramatis personæ*,

" And all goes merry as a marriage bell."

But however good in their way, " dinners"
are habitual only with the " few ;" so we will
think not of " the splendid banquets once a
year," and resign the code of the dining-
room to followers of Brillat-Savarin, Walker,
Ude, and Soyer; the dinner question to
Mrs. Tabitha Tickletooth; and table traits to
Dr. Doran.

Let it not be thought, however, that because some impracticability here presented
itself, and our literary meetings had a strong
and peculiar attraction, we rested in a state of
selfish indifference to the claims of those, who
really constitute the light and life of home;
for, on the contrary, our village evenings, were
marked by many agreeable features, not commanded in the august halls of more remote
localities.

Delightful alike to Spinster and Matron,
Youth and Sage, are the suburban soirées.

Varied in appliances and means of entertainment, Science and Mirth, Sense and Sound—the disciples of Sir David Brewster and Monsieur Jullien—meet upon a common footing. Instruction spreads her most tempting treasures, and Melody sends forth a voice that leaves its dreamy echo long upon the ear.

About eight neighbouring families associated themselves in a *coterie* of this kind, and a double cycle gave a party once a fortnight, from the commencement of winter till the end of spring. They were a little knot of " friends so linked together," that the changes which have taken place, shewing we are but travellers here with no continuing city, would once have seemed incredible, though the moments are still happy when memory photographs their cherished old familiar forms and ruminates on past delights.

The invitations were issued and varied, with a desire to render the meetings accessible to a large circle, but limited, of course, by the capacity of the respective houses ; and although, from the number assembled, these evenings occasionally assumed an air of considerable elegance, the arrangements were ever of the most simple kind.

> " While o'er the light repast
> And sprightly cups they mix in social joy ;
> And through the maze of conversation trace
> Whate'er amuses or improves the mind."

The time of arrival was seven ; at half-past instrumental and vocal music commenced ; objects of art and science were displayed ; or histrionic *morceaux* represented ; and whenever this latter amusement was offered, dramatic talent of high character was evinced. It was *con amore* throughout ; and the *gusto* with which some softening sons of the Society of Friends assumed the Thalian

" sock," afforded a curious antithesis to the demure and tight-laced members of the order.

Then came the usual honours of Terpsichore, which were very generally paid. Philosophers relaxed, and dowagers became sprightly, at the sharp, exhilarating call of the piccolo, though the rapid rotations of the *deux temps*, or the deliberate graces of the Varsoviana, were not to be attempted by those who, like myself, belong to the era of Quadrille. The carpet, (or its damask counterpart,) however, whereon a satin slipper glides, is sacred, and I will only add, that these delightful and rational *réunions*, after a refreshment confined to sandwiches and *gateau*, concluded, before midnight, to the sound of the loyal curfew—" God save the Queen."

This little combination rather promoted

than superseded independent action. It brought into communication some, who, but for its existence, would not have been known to each other; and the example it afforded was not lost upon many, who were frequent guests, without belonging to the body.

At the detached parties not only were later hours kept, but the general arrangements were more liberal; the guests more dressy— sometimes, indeed, going into " costume;"

> " Where all bright hues together run
> In sweet confusion blending."

But let us " Lift not the festal mask;" and vaulting at once from the drawing-room gaieties of Christmas to the *fête champêtres* of Midsummer, echo the sigh of the cavalier—

> " Oh, give me England and July ! "

the only drawback to this otherwise Queen of the Months being her extreme capricity,— balmy and beautiful in the main, but subject to pluvial convulsions, which, in a few impetuous showers, exceed the whole season's labour of Mr. February Fill-Dyke.

The Pic-nic is dependent on the weather, and on the associations of the spot visited;—it wants some memorable site—some ruin, clothed with ivy and strange traditions—such as the

> " cairn and trenched mound,
> Where chiefs of yore sleep lone and sound ;
> And springs, where grey-haired shepherds tell
> That still the Fairies love to dwell ;"

or some long-remembered monarch of the woods,

> " Dark, or with fits of desultory light
> Flung thro' the branches ; "

something of history, poetry, or the pictorial, to awaken, touch, and guide the heart, as in the very enchanting ballad, which at this moment recalls to mind the monument

of Antony Foster I once sketched in an
Oxfordshire church, and the interest with
which Scott invested the victim of the said
Antony's perfidy, Amy Robsart, in his
" Kenilworth," based upon the incidents
recounted in this poem, which has also
received the more recent honor of being followed, in the character of a plaintive mono-
logue which pervades it, by the " Bothwell "
of Professor Aytoun. A few of Mickle's lines,
introducing and following the Lady Amy's
touching soliloquy are transcribed :—

> " The dews of Summer-night did fall ;
>   The Moon—sweet Regent of the sky—
> Silver'd the walls of Cumnor Hall,
>   And many an oak that grew thereby."
> Now nought was heard beneath the skies,
>   The sounds of busy life were still ;
> Save an unhappy lady's sighs,
>   That issued from that lonely pile.

* * * * *

And ere the dawn of day appeared
  In Cumnor Hall, so long and drear,
Full many a piercing scream was heard,
  And many a cry of mortal fear.
The death-bell thrice was heard to ring,
  An aerial voice was heard to call;
And thrice the raven flapped his wing
  Around the towers of Cumnor Hall.

* * * * *

The village maids, with fearful glance,
  Avoid the ancient moss-grown wall,
Nor ever lead the merry dance
  Among the groves of Cumnor Hall.
Full many a traveller oft hath sighed,
  And pensive wept the Countess' fall,
As wandering onward they 've espied
  The haunted towers of Cumnor Hall."

With fine weather, and the intellect of a large party thus aroused, the *al fresco* becomes most enjoyable, and would require a modern Chaucer to describe—a Watteau to depict it.

The considerate owners of many interesting relics lay them open to Pic-nicians ; and among the very charming spots for primæval quietude and romantic scenery thus rendered occasionally accessible to Londoners, may be noticed Lord Ellesmere's, St. George's Hill, near Weybridge, Surrey.

> Can Kent design like Nature?   Mark where Thames
> Plenty and pleasure pours thro' Lincoln's meads.
> Can the great artist, tho' with taste supreme
> Endued, one beauty to this Eden add?

But lest I be thought to possess an over-weening relish for feasts, and to pursue trifling objects with more ardour than a foxhunter, paying early vows to pleasure and rising but to " Waken Lords and Ladies gay ;" it may be worth while to note that we are expressly permitted, or even enjoined, to taste of honey when we find it : Saul and Jonathan were pleasant in their lives : our senators are not always engrossed

with "leets and law days:" Lord Chancellors
find time for vacation rambles; and none
enjoy a recreative hour so keenly as those
who are most sedulous in their ordinary
vocations. "A merry heart goes all the
day, your sad tires in a mile a." Besides,
a due attention to such things is strictly
accordant with the versatile nature of
the Architect's vocation—a point on which
Sir William Chambers (our best modern
master) observes, with grave and forcible
coincidence, "He, furthermore, must be well
versed in the customs, ceremonies, and modes
of life of all degrees of men, his contem-
poraries, their occupations and amusements,
the number and employments of their domes-
tics, equipages, and appurtenances, in what
manner the business allotted to each is performed, and what is requisite or proper to
facilitate the service, with many other particu-
lars, which, though seemingly trifling, must
not be unknown to him who is to provide for

the wants, and gratify the expectations of all ;"
and this little sketch has seemed necessary,
to mark the fact that changes of no mean
importance are taking place around us, and
society is acquiring a basis upon which
it could not have stood at any earlier
period.

Upon the governing bias of this transition
rest, indeed, considerations of deep interest
for the future.   There is a most important
field laid open to female influence; and, in
order that this influence be rightly directed,
a careful training of the female mind becomes
imperative.   Frankness, unselfishness, mode-
ration—Truth and fortitude—are all within
its scope; and to the promulgation of these
principles, rather than to the pleasant
arts of pleasing in the fair princesses of
creation, we must look for noble citizens;
for a race of that high-souled and manly
stamp, who, with a full sense of duty,

appreciate good government, and constitute
the brightest subjects, the proudest bulwarks,
of a realm !

If the child be father to the man,
so is the mental seed impressed upon the
plastic brain of early life the parent of
its future fruit. Let not, then, the want of
judgment, in the sower mar the grand result,
but let the moral education of females keep
pace with that general advance of instruction
which promises such rapid and important
effects. Not only are our chief Universities
about to adjust themselves to modern wants,
but, besides giving their social passports to
the world, to become really beacons of high
intelligence. To this movement we owe the
middle-class examinations, which have set all
the Dominies throughout the country on their
metal. Merit in the civil service claims equal
rights with Patronage, and even Generals
disdain not the olive wreath of science. We

have training colleges not only for cadets and subalterns, but for staff officers—so that to the list of graduates in other faculties, may some day be added that of Doctor in War!

Why, then, should a matter of such deep and vital importance to every family as the training of its young gentlewomen, be thought worthy of no further care than the provision of a governess, aided, it may be, by professors of eminence, for all the so-called accomplishments? Are they to be thus prepared for the creditable performance of life's duties, and a due fulfilment of the higher objects of existence? Will the next generation owe to them—as it ought to do, if we are to advance—more than they have received from their predecessors? Will it find them more generally "women of worth," oftener "mothers of great men?" Will their employments surpass those of ladies in the seventeenth century, or the "angel in the house" more commonly displace the "animated doll?" Will "a woman's preachings" have had their full effect on woman's practice or will " My life, and what shall I do with it?" be as generally considered and profited by as "an old maid" would desire, or rather shall we say as would meet and satisfy the " aspirations" of the philanthropic and the wise ?

I fear the answer must be too uniformly, No. But the public mind having been somewhat generally and forcibly appealed to, the field of woman's worth will not much longer lie a neglected fallow, though the too-severe charge of mental *severance* may, and ought to, be at once repelled.

How tenderly, reverently, and faithfully wealthy ladies often feel and perform duties to their Creator, themselves, and their fellows, the church, the school, the wayside conduit, and the "Home" for aged, hoary heads, will help to shew; and that the same high principles exist where wealth has been withheld, it would be absurd to doubt; but the whole vast sisterhood has to be enlisted on the side of improvement, and employed in the field of general advancement.

And as to our complaining and reclusive celibitators, they know not that for all the sacrifices that tear the pursestrings and overthrow all notions of self-preservation, poor Benedict finds a welcome and a fair return, as Mr. Patmore can explain :—

> " For, somehow, he whose daily life
> Adapts itself to one true wife,
> Grows to a nuptial near degree,
> With all's that's fair and womanly."

But what have I written? Is it fixed as that of Pontius?—shall it be effaced as if inscribed in sand?—or shall it be followed by a *misericorde?* Yes, thus it shall be. Not for fear of shells and pointed bullets from Sandhurst, vulnerable though I be in every part, and not, like Achilles, only in the *heel;* and would that I were

> " Only weak
> Against the charm of Beauty's powerful glance ; "

but it does seem becoming to explain, that it is not proposed to send the Schoolmaster among the ladies, to render them wiser by making them less charming; the variety of study here suggested being well suited to win hearts, and of more perdurable worth than many accomplishments tied up with the hymeneal knot, and never 'woke again.

At dinner once, I had placed a lady on my right, opposite to a Reverend Doctor, who, happening to make some good-humoured allusion to an incident in Eden, was retorted upon by his fair *vis-à-vis,* " Ah, Adam was a

sneak !" Now, I would not be Adam for ever
so much. The little melody of " Ah, no—I'll
not believe it," converted into a taunt, would
wound me deeply. I will never prove a
recreant ; but, like Ulysses' poor brute,
Argus, (named after an architect, by-the-
bye,) be faithful to the end,— *loyal au
mort.*

Social education for girls, then ; heavy
fines on rich bachelors ; and " A House for
the Suburbs" for ever !—that is, until its fair
occupants are removed to a brighter abode,
a better mansion prepared by the Great
Architect—a house not made with hands—
eternal in the Heavens !

Very distinct is modern society from that
of former periods ; very superior our condition
in regard to the security of property and
person ; and altogether unprecedented our

rapidity of locomotion;—yet the character
of our dwellings is, or ought to be, equally
distinguishable from those of any previous
age.

In the early times of Greece and Italy,
the house was contained within a walled
boundary, without windows, the enclosure
being divided into courts, and the rooms
constructed against the walls of these courts,
leaving the central portions open for light
and air. The only difference between the
town and country domicile being the existence of an extra court or two in the
latter case, for cattle and the preparation of
oil and wine, though the distinction afterwards expanded. But no organization of a
former world, revealed by the labours of the
Geologist, surpasses in wonder the even
parodoxical means by which a perfect knowledge of a Roman house of the first century

has been obtained—namely, the destruction or overwhelming of the cities of Herculaneum and Pompeii by the ashes of Mount Vesuvius, —a knowledge so admirably illustrated at the Crystal Palace; and no description of the original is more acceptable than that in " The Last Days."

Each group of buildings, surrounded by streets, was called an island ; and one of these attracted great interest at the time of its discovery, from the singular and beautiful nature of the decorations. The island contained four houses, and the one selected for description is called that of the Dramatic Poet.

"You enter by a long and narrow vestibule[1], on the floor of which is the image of a dog in mosaic, with the well-known ' Cave canem,' or ' Beware of the dog.' On either side is a chamber of some size[2], for the

interior part of the house not being large
enough to contain the two great divisions of
private and public apartments; these two
rooms were set apart for the reception of
visitors who neither by rank nor familiarity
were entitled to admission in the penetralia of
the mansion.

"Advancing up the vestibule, you enter an
atrium[(3)], that,
when first dis-
covered, was
rich in paint-
ings, which, *in
point of expres-
sion*, would
scarcely dis-
grace a Raffa-
elle. You may
see them now
transplanted to

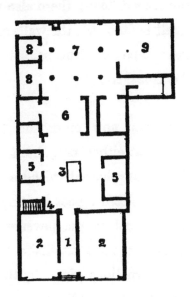

the Neapolitan Museum; they are still the

admiration of connoisseurs ; they depict the parting of Achilles and Brisëis. Who does not acknowledge the force, the vigour, the beauty, employed in delineating the forms and faces of Achilles and the immortal slave ?

" On one side the atrium(4), a small staircase admitted to the apartments for the slaves on the second floor ; there also were two or three small bedrooms(5), the walls of which portrayed the Rape of Europa, the Battle of the Amazons, &c.

" You now enter the tablinum(6), across which, at either end, hung rich draperies of Tyrian purple, half withdrawn. On the walls were depicted a poet reciting his verses to his friends, and in the pavement was inserted a small and most exquisite mosaic, typical of the instructions given by the director of the stage to his comedians.

" You passed through this saloon and entered the peristyle[7], and here (as I have said before was usually the case with the smaller houses of Pompeii) the mansion ended. From each of the seven columns that adorned the court hung festoons of garlands; the centre, supplying the place of a garden, bloomed with the rarest flowers, placed in vases of white marble that were supported on pedestals. At the left hand of this small garden was a diminutive fane resembling one of those small chapels placed at the side of roads in Catholic countries, and dedicated to the Penates. Before it stood a bronze tripod; to the left of the colonnade were two small cubicula, or bed rooms[8], to the right was the triclinium[9], or dining room."

We do not however, enjoy the balmy airs of Greece or the Bay of Naples. We do not live in courts, but have literally turned the house inside out, since the days of Vitruvius,

who gives some advice on adapting habitations to climate. " In cold climates," he says,
" and in regions remote from the South, the
heat is not sufficiently powerful to effect the
dispersion of vapours; on this account the
atmosphere is charged with damps and causes
an accumulation of the humours of the
system, by which the body is rendered
corpulent and the tones of the voice bass.
From this cause it happens that the inhabitants of Northern regions have a large stature
and fair complexions, their hair straight and
red! bah!"

We Englishmen are not a red-haired race,
albeit we have had a rufine king and many
worthy examples of that chromatic tendency,
but they must be regarded rather as an
interesting variety than the normal represen-
tatives of the species, therefore good Marcus
Pollio, adieu! return to thy repose and the
shades of those whose minds of fire and limbs

of force have secured their passage through all ages, and of those daughters of heroic sires whose symmetry of form and purity of soul have made them meet companions of the blest,

" Who ever new, not subject to decays,
    Spread and grow brighter with the length of days,"

while I consult more humble but more practical sources of information.

The manor-house of the eleventh, twelfth, and thirteenth centuries seems to have been a parallelogram of two stories, the lower vaulted and not communicating with the upper (in which was the only fire-place), the steps being outside. A square tower for greater safety was sometimes attached, and the great hall, the turret stair, and other innovations were gradually introduced; but it was after the wars of the Roses, and the coalition of the factious houses of York and Lancaster, by Henry the Seventh's marriage

with the Princess Elizabeth, and the further
important union of England and Scotland
under James I., or at least of the imminent
prospect of that union in Queen Elizabeth's
time, that our domestic architecture assumed
any close approximation to its present
character.

Mansions in the Virgin reign were most
commonly formed on the plan of her initial
—**E,** and were therefore symmetrical externally. The chief alteration, in point of
style, has been due to the influx of Italian
details and treatment ; and, in point of *plan*,
to the varying habits of the day; and this
cause is as active now as ever. No architectural quality of a dwelling conduces so
extensively to the satisfaction and comfort of
its occupants as a well-contrived Plan ;—and
nothing is more inconvenient in result than ill-
considered or misconceived arrangements. I
have been painfully conscious of this in

making some alterations to an ancestral
edifice in Berkshire, where the whole
arrangement is left-handed; the best and
warmer aspects being occupied by offices
and stables, while the family rooms are
confined to the biting North and East,—
a defect that can only be alleviated at considerable cost, and never entirely overcome.

Bacon rightly enough prefers utility to
ornament, and says, "Let use be preferred
before uniformity, except where both may
be had. Houses," he need not have told
us, "are built to live in;" and when he
adds, "not to look on," he registers a mis-
take. Houses form a component of the
period's costume, like the habiliments, the
carriages, and all the items of taste. To
"leave, then, the goodly fabrics of houses
for beauty only to the enchanted palaces
of the poets, who build them with small
cost," is to close up one great source of

H

enjoyment, and to pass a censure upon bounteous Nature, who not provides alone for every turn of service, but superadds the mould of grace—the exquisite in colour !

Although neither Vitruvius nor Bacon impart the precise information now required, the former teaches that buildings ought to be adapted to climate as well as to specific uses ; and Bacon, living comparatively among us, approaches the subject with corresponding exactitude, and it seems possible to reconcile his precepts with all that modern objects and correct taste demand.

If for uniformity, or that strict symmetry of arrangement which dictates the recurrence of the same forms, we substitute the PICTORIAL style, we shall not only attain to the combination of the useful and the beautiful—the *utile et dulce*—but do so by means more strictly accordant with Nature's own method ; securing the effect of *balance*, *stability*, and *repose*, by the counterpoise of masses similar in capacity, but varying in form, and allowing full scope for finish and detail,—yet ever dreading, and sedulously avoiding, the trifling *higgledy-piggledy* manner, whose puerilities, carried to an extremity in some ecclesiastical works, cast a retrograding stigma on the 'scutcheon of Art.

It is impossible to peruse Lord Bacon's Essays without improvement, and I shall only, and with due respect, close the tome of that same learned Theban, to come at once to the floating experience of the present generation, which may be presumed to exist principally among the Architects now practising.

The archives of this studio alone record a great (perhaps unprecedented) number of dwellings built during the last fifteen years, for men of great mental acquirement and refined feeling, though of moderate pecuniary endowment ; and, from the careful revisal of the plans submitted to so purifying an ordeal, I may well hope to extract something suited to our immediate purpose, and by throwing their varied claims into review,

" Choose a firm cloud before it fall, and in it
  Catch, ere she change, the Cynthia of the minute."

Dimensions whether large or small, have but slight influence, it may be stated, on the merit of a design. Fitness and beauty are almost independent of size, just as a miniature may be more excellent than a kit-cat. " The house of Glaucus was at once one of the smallest and yet one of the most adorned and finished of all the private mansions of Pompeii ; it would be a model at this day for the house of a single man in May Fair, the envy and despair of the cœlebian purchasers of buhl and marquetry."

The little mansion (near Wimbledon Park) of which the site plan is given, was conceived in a spirit that may perhaps humbly reflect the feeling of some modern Glaucus, though the arrangements differ from the Pompeian mode as diametrically as would the modern exquisite from his ancient prototype.

The public road is on the South; the enclosure, a simple wall without ornament or opening except at the entrance, which is marked by bold piers. Carriage and foot gates, are supported by strong oak posts with moulded terminations; for it is an error to hang gates, though small, to piers of brick or stone, however large, as the jar is sure to fracture and destroy the rigid and unresilient mass. The drive conducts you to the house[1], whose entrance is marked by the external lamp[9], and then goes on to the stable[2] and kitchen court[11], by the turn necessitated by the elevated mound which at once conceals some inferior depositories, and supplies dry slopes for sweet-scented herbs, as well as lofty trees screening, perhaps, some undesired object beyond, and securing the pleasure to be obtained by changing levels as well as by varying directions. The shrubs by which this drive is hedged are mostly evergreen, and dense enough to preclude an oversight of the adjacent space.

The house door, it will be noticed, is on the East, and the vestibule, hall, study, and dining room, are the only family apartments on the ground story, an arrangement by which the plan is kept within moderate bounds, and the drawing room is increased in importance by the ornamental character of the staircase by which it is approached, a more ample view is obtained, and the golden rays of the evening sun are felt till they sink into the deep absorbing grey of night.

You pass no other room to arrive at this,
but a gallery leads to bed-chambers on the
same level. There are no rooms above; and,
as there is no basement or under-ground
story, an inquiry may arise as to where the
servants' bedrooms are ?—they are neither on
the ground or one-pair, but between, in a
mezzanine entresol, or *half-story,* as commonly adopted on the Continent, and obtained
by giving only the necessary height to larders
and the smaller offices; but the kitchen is, as
it ought to be, a lofty apartment.

The windows of the dining room open
upon a terrace[8], flanked by the conservatory[3],
and ornamented with vases of suitable plants.
From this terrace a few steps lead down to the
flower garden [7], and the lawns [6], which are also
edged with beds of bulbous or other flowering
roots; the verge is dotted with roses and
other deciduous standards, selected chiefly to
please the eye, but without prejudice to such
as also bear something ultimately beneficial.

PLAN

OF

THE SITE OF A HOUSE,

OR

MANSIONETTE,

NEAR

WIMBLEDON PARK, SURREY.

———◆———

1.—House.

2.—Stables.

3.—Conservatory.

4.—Vinery.

5. ⎫
   ⎬ Lawns.
5. ⎭

6.—Kitchen Garden.

7.—Flower Garden.

8.—Terrace.

9.—Lamp.

10.—Stable Yard.

11.—Kitchen Court.

12.—Jet d'Eau.

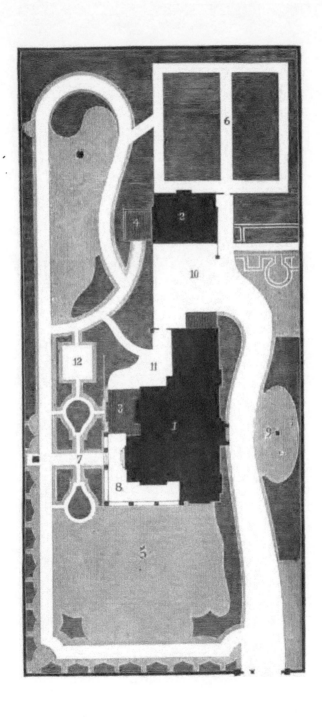

On the northern lawn stands a forest elm, under the grateful shade of which the summer air is breathed with sensuous delight. Mounds again afford shelter; and, though out of sight, not wholly out of mind, there is the little kitchen garden.   System, however, is seldom more serviceable than in horticulture. An experienced nurseryman once told me that he could make a useful garden in a space not larger than a butcher's tray, and I therefore resign the subject to professional skill.

Mr. Rivers, of Sawbridgeworth, has done so much to demonstrate and improve the management of small gardens, as to entitle him to the thanks of every suburban amateur.   By a clever process of dwarfing he obtains from low pyramidal trees and bushes, and from walls only four feet high, luxurious crops of out-door fruit, perfect in form, size, and flavour *.

* Details are given in an explanatory manual published by Messrs. Longman.

I will now explain the plan illustrating a
pair of semi-detached houses, designed for an
estate under my professional care, where it is
proposed to give to each residence about a
quarter of an acre of land.

We have here a " party wall," or division,
common to both houses. This wall is necessarily without windows, but fireplaces may be
conveniently placed against it, and occasion
may be here taken to

> " Look to the towered chimneys which should be
>   The windpipes of good hospitality,"

as Bishop Hall opined, but which have more
commonly been classed among domestic
plagues. Yet the good bishop has not been
wholly alone, for a namesake of mine sings
merrily the chimney's praise.

> " But a house is much more to my taste than a tree,
>   And for groves, O ! a good grove of chimneys for me !"

The ruins of Rochester Castle afford a very early instance of the recessed fireplace with a short flue rising only a few feet, and emitting the smoke through the surface of the wall; but the superior efficacy of the lengthened tunnel reaching to the roof was soon afterwards discovered and adopted, though the mode of heating large houses by charcoal fires in open iron grates has been retained occasionally almost down to our own day. A rude and primitive way indeed, but more efficacious than any substituted plan for warming by the open fire, for in that case all the heat evolved from the fuel was received by the atmosphere, while in more recent contrivances three parts of it has been lost— nay, often continues to be, despite the efforts of Count Romford and our own Doctor Arnott.

We cannot go back to the pan of charcoal (except indeed as a *last* resource), and though we can no longer have fires in the centre of our apartments, we may arrange them to a considerable extent in the centre of our houses, so that the heat may be to the largest degree retained within them. Flues of greater height may usually be obtained in the interior than in the outer walls, and nothing looks worse or betrays defect more thoroughly than a chimney rising from the eaves of a roof to a disproportionate height, and then surmounted by that preposterous abortion, a " tall-boy." Chimneys are indeed more capricious than aught else in the whole category of structural circumstances —in some cases nothing seems to prevent a draught, and in others it appears unattainable —still let it ever be kept in mind where a choice is open, that fire places are best in inner walls, long tunnels are better than short, and that as to form, straight flues are inferior in efficacy to such as are carried obliquely, converting them in point of fact into *reflectors* of the passing caloric, and thus raising the temperature and aiding the upward current of the smoke. This system demands a wall of somewhat more than " speculative " thickness, but the extra cost would be saved over and over again by precluding the hideous remedies which proclaim our parsimony and want of skill so loudly and offensively in every street and building.

Flues then should be constructed on the principle of REFLECTION, and in grates the property of NON-CONDUCTION is best secured by the thick clay or earthenware backs now coming into general use; and if a further word may be allowed, I would mention that in the house already described, the chimneys of the best rooms are swept from the kitchen, by which much dirt and injury to furniture is prevented.

With these preliminary remarks let us step up to the door which gives admission to the entrance hall, an adjunct which ought never to be omitted, as the privacy and comfort of the whole house may be said to depend on its existence.   Adjoining the hall is the study or " master's " room, next to this is the drawing room for lady visitors, morning calls, and evening use, and more retired is the *salle à manger*, the dining room adjacent to the stairs, and allowing the easy service of dinner without crossing the guests.   Most ladies know the value of a small store room in this quarter, and a wash-hand place for gentlemen completes the ground or principal floor.

This design has, of course, its basement, or sub-story, giving ample room for kitchen, scullery, larders, and a good housekeeper's room, to be fitted with drawers, presses, and shelves, which are never more appreciated than when, as is commonly and commendably the case in small establishments, the lady, in the phraseology of the advertisements, " is her own housekeeper."

Upstairs, each story would comprise four bed-rooms, a dressing-room, and water-closet.

PLAN OF A PAIR OF SEMI-DETACHED HOUSES.

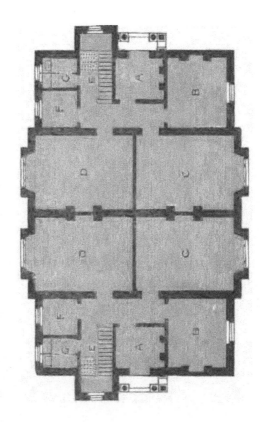

A.—Hall.   B.—Study.   C.—Drawing Room.   D.—Dining Room.
E.—Staircase.   F.—Storeroom.   G.—Wash-hand Room, with W.C.

SEMI-DETACHED HOUSES.

PLAN

OF

A COMPACT HOUSE NEAR BLACKHEATH.

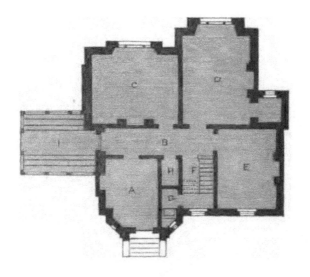

A.—Hall.   E.—Study.

B.—Lobby.   F.—Stairs.

C.—Drawing Room.   G.—Water Closet.

D.—Dining Room.   H.—Cupboard.

I.—Conservatory.

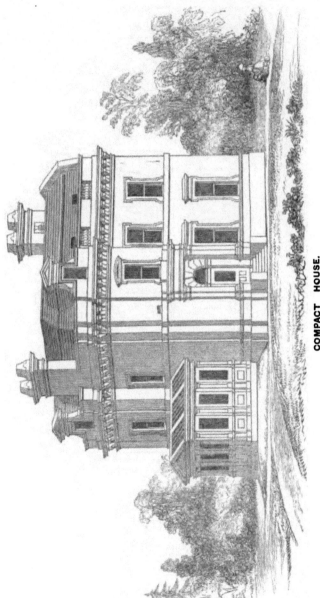

COMPACT HOUSE.

The preceding plan and sketch illustrate a compact house, of modern Italian character, recently built for a lady near Blackheath, Kent; and although the site does not exceed a quarter of an acre, the house is fully detached, and the garden, being wholly ornamental and well kept, is found to be sufficient.

The entrance hall and the study face the East, the dining and drawing rooms look to the West, and the conservatory forms a very agreeable addition on the South. Under the dining room and study are the kitchen and scullery; the larder and wine cellar come under the hall; and beneath the drawing room is a very serviceable apartment, fitted with presses and a bath. There are four bed-rooms (with a water closet) on the first floor; and the number might have been repeated above, but two only were required.

A consideration of the foregoing plan

will preclude the necessity of much further explanation to demonstrate the fact that the same space in family apartments and the same extent of servants' offices in a house without a basement, requires just double the ground occupied where the under story exists; but the advantage of spreading the plan over the necessary superficies is soon acknowledged where the extent of land admits the choice. We shall now, therefore, give attention to a design on the country plan, or that which seems best adapted to " a House for the Suburbs," and first the Glebe House.

This design contains the accommodation usually required where the benefice is a Perpetual Curacy or small Vicarage and would of course suit the family of a layman adopting a similar scale of expenditure.

THE GLEBE HOUSE, GROUND PLAN.

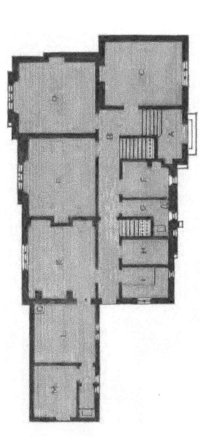

A.—Vestibule.   D.—Drawing Room.   G.—Wash-hand Room.   K.—Kitchen.
B.—Staircase.   E.—Dining Room.   H.—Cellar.   L.—Scullery.
C.—Study.   F.—Store Room.   I.—Larder.   M.—Coals.

THE GLEBE HOUSE.

Our purpose to build now losing its former vagueness and becoming more settled and definite, justifies some inquiry concerning the usages of the building arts, and the first step of all must be to place ourselves in the hands of an experienced adviser. So

> " Call up him that left half told
> The story of Cambuscan bold."

Or stay,—lest he be rife with bastions, battlements, and donjon-keeps,—let's rather bid a thousand times good-morrow to kind Sir Eglinour,

> " Upon whose faith and honour I repose."

The terms Architect and Surveyor are commonly accepted as mere synonimes, like Solicitor and Attorney, the first in each case being the more complimentary and grateful; but a closer demarcation defines the province of the architect by taste, design, and science, and gives to the other commercial questions

and accounts; but the two departments
are often combined in the same professor.
The architect charges for his services,
extending to the preparation (and use,
but not the property or copyright) of
drawings, specifications, and general supervision of works, the uniform rate of five per
cent. on the outlay, which is by no means
remunerative in small and intricate buildings,
though satisfactory enough it may be in
palaces, museums, and other colossal works,
to which it is equally extended, for the cases
of officers to public bodies enjoying some
prescription or monopoly, paid partly by
salaries or retaining fees, and partly by a
reduced commission, are not analogous; nor
can the recent contest in regard to the Palace
of Parliament be viewed as an authoritative
precedent, even where the expenditure is
extraordinary.

The parsimony that would curtail convenience is certainly ill-judged, but to be over-housed is at once to render a fortune too small, and the importance of the proper scale justifies the greatest circumspection. Lord Bacon, as we have seen, gives cautions against castle building, and whether the recent suspicion of his lordship's hand in Shakspeare's works be correct or not, they also convey the soundest precepts; thus he of Avon says:—

> " Shouldst we survey
> The plot of situation and the model,
> Consent upon a sure foundation,
> Question Surveyors; know our own estate,
> How able such a work to undergo;"

and reiterates the principle by deeming the incautious

> " Like one that draws the model of a house
> Beyond his power to build it up; who half through
> Gives o'er and leaves his part-created cost,
> A naked subject to the weeping clouds,
> And waste for churlish winter's tyranny."

Which seems as plain an exhortation to

K

adopt the system of contracts and estimates as could be given by the gravest of modern jurists.

It is doubtless very salutary to count the cost before entering upon an expenditure of magnitude, and it occasions the builder no more trouble to prepare an estimate beforehand than to make out a bill at the completion of his work; and either task may be regarded as an item of prime cost, or a tax upon profits, at will; but, when it happens that competitive tenders from several builders are desired, it is customary for these gentlemen to assemble, on the architect's invitation, and appoint a practitioner, exclusively employed in such business, to "extract the quantities," as it is termed, and place before the parties who employ him a correct representation of the amount of work of each kind, and all the conditions and circumstances affecting it; so that the only open question is that of *price*,—a limitation which sometimes keeps the amount of tenders very close to each other, but in others fails to preclude immense disparity. Such points, however, are chiefly worth notice for the purpose of dispelling the nonsense written on the subject, and to shew that, beyond the legitimate extent of his designs and specification, it would be most inexpedient and dangerous for an architect to interfere in such competitions.

The disappointment sometimes experienced with regard to expense arises in a great measure from nursing too fondly a first impression formed at the very outset of affairs, instead of allowing that impression to expand with extended purposes and improved ideas. Houses of similar size may differ very much in cost, from mere embellishment and fitting up, but when a room has been enlarged here, a desirable feature added there, and all the circumstances of *time* and place brought into view, how utterly erroneous may the figures set down appear? Within my own experience, plans, identical in every respect, have been executed for eight hundred pounds in one place and have cost half as much more in another; therefore nothing short of a builder's tender can be properly deemed a reliable estimate. From this reason and the obvious impropriety of disclosing the cost of private houses, I abstained in the first edition from all such representations; but as some criterion appears to be desired, a few cases, analogous in several respects, may be put forward.

Parsonages are of a semi-public nature, and those erected by the Ecclesiastical Commission constitute a peculiar and valuable class of dwellings, widely spread through England and Wales. They were built under conditions precluding all display, but admitting substantial construction and completeness of arrangement.

These houses have three living rooms, kitchen, scullery, store pantry, larder, cellar, and an outhouse on the ground floor, with half-a-dozen bed rooms and water closet on the one pair. The dining and drawing rooms are sixteen by fourteen feet each, and the study twelve feet square; the walls of local stone or brick, and the divisions are solid walls. Slating is generally used for the roofs. They are in fact strong, well-timbered, untrembling houses, likely to stand for ages with but little attention. They are amply fitted with joinery, marble and stone chimney pieces, register grates, range, dresser, copper boiler, bells, and sometimes a brick oven. A well and force-pump, a cesspool, and drains are also among the provisions; but fencing and laying out the ground were not included. The average value of such buildings is about eleven hundred pounds, with a margin of fifty for contingencies as at Hoxton, Stepney, Muswell Hill, Rotherhithe, Richmond, Uxbridge, God-

stsone, Foot's Cray, &c. near London, and
others in the denser seats of provincial population.

Another group partly under private patronage would include such as the Italian House
at Hambridge, Somerset, the town-like example
at Rotherham, and those other Tudor instances
of more extended plan and country character
at Meanwood, near Leeds, Esh by Durham,
Lenton at Nottingham, Lingfield, Surrey, &c.
giving an average of seventeen hundred
pounds. More liberal means were here at
command, stables were occasionally needed,
and increased attention allowed to style in
which they commonly present the light Italian,
our modern vernacular though too severely
simple mode. That of the Tudor and
Jacobean periods was occasionally employed
though it may be regretted that the caution
exercised over the funds seems to have
repressed artistic effort and precluded much

play of composition or variety of feature ; but
when the mellowing influence of Time shall
have softened the crudities of new materials,
stippled the walls with lichens, wreathed clim-
bers about the chimney shafts, taught birds,
those feathered choristers, to warble forth their
ariel matin-song acceptable to every faith from
eaves and corners, and roses to struggle for
admission at every window, the hearts within
these modest houses may have much reason
to be grateful for the early labours of the
Ecclesiastical Commission while the abandon-
ment of centralization for local supervision
must (at least I hope so) enhance the benefits
of its future workings.

But it is necessary to say that, as the conditions and interests of clerical incumbency
differ from those of ordinary proprietorship,
the parsonage scarcely offers to the skill of
the architect that full opportunity for con-
trasting effect with cost, which is so welcome

under freer circumstances, and so rapid is the transition of architectural sentiment, that it would be unfair to speak of almost any houses though but a few years old in any other respect than as grounds of experience and criterions of expense.

The "Glebe House" suited to a perpetual curacy might be erected as a low-roofed villa for thirteen hundred pounds, but would cost a hundred and fifty or two hundred more in " the parcel wood and parcel stone" manner shewn in the sketch.

The " semi-detached houses," plainly finished, may be estimated at fourteen hundred pounds each ; the " compact house," with greenhouse, and a thorough fitting up, with bath and fixtures, about fifteen hundred pounds ; and the " House for the Suburbs," with its appurtenances, must be set down approximately at three thousand.

Architectural style is a point deserving a few, though simply passing remarks, in direct affinity with our subject. A House for the Suburbs is obviously free from the more exact treatment of the Town Mansion, yet is placed far above mere rude and negligent rusticity. It is a natural and laudable impulse, which gives priority in choice to native features, without excluding the agreeable modifications and adventitious graces derivable from foreign observation,— so that our buildings are governed by the rule that operates in men, and renders those most worthy of imitation who have picked up items of character at many points, and blended them into one acceptable whole—not too straight, or *point device*,— everywhere at ease—and not leaders of fashion, or far behind it.

" They 're not the first by whom the New are tried,
  Nor yet the last to lay the Old aside."

The insecurity which made strength so exclusive a consideration down to the close of Henry VI. had been succeeded by a gradual change in political circumstances; and architecture was not slow in assuming the improvements available from augmented intercourse and more intimate continental relationship; and the " prodigal bravery in building" attained in the time of Elizabeth is especially noticed by Camden, "verily, to the great ornament of the kingdom," though he simultaneously complains of the concomitant " riotous banquetting, " and the decay of the " glorious hospitality of the nation."

The innovations in building at that time occurred most rapidly; the chief elements of modern houses were introduced; and, from the engrafting of Italian scions on the old Gothic stock, arose that picturesque hybrid, which, not wholly indigenous nor altogether exotic, we cheerfully accept as a national variety of Art.

It may be divested of uniformity with unimpaired effect; the joint employment of brick and stone is an agreeable characteristic; and the interior decorations may be applied with a sparing or more liberal hand; while the predominating quaintness, the slight infusion of the grotesque, is favourable to richness, and a foil to criticism.

The reaction in favour of Gothic art matured in a great degree by the felicitous pencils of Blore, Pugin, and Scott, has been occasionally perverted into a sort of pre-Anglican counterpart of the pre-Raphaelite in painting. There is an example at W * * * where neither in church, school, or parsonage, a single feature calls to mind that a dynasty of Tudors have existed, or that the

great event of Henry's life ever took place,
and light continues to be shed from the lamp
maker's version of a Papal tiara! This is not
in an edifice where Catholicism is openly and
faithfully professed and taught, but one within
the pale " by law established." The architect,
of course, simply fulfilled his instructions and
gained the credit due to a beautiful work;
but it is the petrifaction of an enigma such as
the Synagogues of the Israelites would afford
if built in the Egyptian manner. We should
ask whether they pined for a return to bond-
age or preserved a warning memento of the
thraldom they had escaped. Between the
Roman and the Reformed Churches a practical
cordiality prevails while the sub-classes of
Protestantism are vexed by doctrinal asperi-
ties and petty persecutions.

I do not share the exaggerated apprehension of a late venerable prelate, that the battle
of the Reformation will have to be fought

again; nothing human is perfect, and to deny
the possibility of improvement is against the
principle of our kind mother church, but
wholesome progress may be checked by pre-
mature display and indiscreet excess. Allow-
ance can be freely made for varying opinions;
but it is sufficiently painful to see the purest
efforts to impart the blessings of instruction
regarded as disengenuous sectarian attempts
from the mere form of building adopted, so
much has the battle of the styles become
identified with that deplorable and retrogres-
sive battle of the creeds, by which civilization
is retarded, the bond of peace shaken, and the
household of faith divided and scandalized.

In throwing off a condition of sloth it was
not necessary that zealous churchmen should
adopt a style of rank exotic mediævalism; and
though Miriam's loud timbrel and the healing
melody of David's harp may fitly swell the
pealing anthem and the grateful hymn, choral

deprecation is as inferior to the untutored trembling accents of prayerful hearts as would be the frantic lamentations of hired mourners to the holy sob of heartfelt love, whose tear bedews and sanctifies the grave.

The best thing resulting from this conflict is an enlarged study of continental buildings, whether south of the Tiber or northward of the Rhine, by which a new impetus has been given and a new field laid open to architectural design, enabling us by the substitution of coloured materials and surface decoration for forms, heretofore produced only in relief, to combine increased effect with diminished expenditure, as the dash of the scene painter may be often acceptable where we cannot command the patient finish of an easel picture.

Viewing style as an element of expense, it may be said, that the practice of design, is interesting in proportion to the degree, in

which the distinguishing peculiarities are
allowed to be developed; and it is degree,
rather than manner, that regulates expense.
In "gothic," a certain amount of architectural feature, demanding masonry and carved
stone or wood work, is permitted; while the
term " Italian" is too commonly applied where
every possible abstraction of richness has been
made.

When the Vicarage at Gretton, in Rutland-
shire, was to be built, it was ascertained, by
a very careful process, that the adoption of
a gothic design would have increased the
cost from fourteen hundred to sixteen hundred pounds.   It therefore seems hardly
admissible for architects to talk of practising
in one exclusive style, as it must occasionally
force upon a client that which may be very
expensive to him, though agreeable enough
to the designer, and oblige him to accept
rhyme, when he only asks—ah! me—for rea-

son; though, having studied English architecture with long and zealous attention, I may add, "for the labour we delight in physics pain," I have no preference for other modes of building.

The selection of building materials is a subject worth the gravest attention; a care, indeed, that is not rendered less onerous by the great variety open to the choice, whether coming direct from the mineral and organic stores of Nature, the furnace of the metallurgist, the kiln of the potter, or other manipulative sources.

How saddening is it to see some magnificent edifice, while proclaiming the energy and genius united in its conception, revealing also the germ of wasting disease, and branded with the sentence of destruction ere it well leaves the hands of its designer ; but

such things have ever been, and seem
destined to continue, in defiance of all
human precautions.

In the pure air of the "sweet South,"
indeed, the process of disintegration is imperceptible, except by the micrometry of hoary
epochs; but here, in "the tyrannous breathing
of the North," the progress of corrosion and
decay is hasty and unsparing.

The rapid decomposition of the stone used
in the Palace of Westminster (that wonderful
adaptation of an Italian skeleton and a Gothic
skin) has been the subject of much recent
animadversion, and the wretched expedient of
preventive washes has been resorted to but
fortunately without success. The action of
disease is partial, and, curiously enough, confined to portions least exposed to the free
influence of the weather, a circumstance that
negatives the notion of unusually hurtful

L

ingredients in the London atmosphere. The
absurdity of applying a general remedy to a
merely topical evil must speak for itself,
and a further absurdity is that of expecting
any preventive wash to possess the res-
torative power of re-converting into solid
stone that which has once disintegrated and
mouldered away. The rational plan would
seem to be to remove all infected surfaces
and make good with a veneering of stone
especially prepared, or a stone-resembling
stucco, of whose durability there shall be
good assurance. In this way the original
appearance may be retained and the reproach
of a palace of compo averted.

The employment of concrete, an imitation of
conglomerate rock or pudding stone, has been
very advantageous in foundations, becoming at
once incompressible, and imparting uniformity
to soils of unequal character. When dry, it
acquires the property of a beam; but this

comes gradually, according to the mass, a circumstance not always sufficiently considered, so that in some works now in progress the depth of concrete is said to be from ten to twenty feet, and will probably not be fully indurated during the present century. Besides being used in the trenches beneath the walls, it may be advantageously spread, to a moderate thickness, over the whole area of a building.

Bricks are of such venerable antiquity, that it is impossible to forget their extensive use by the Egyptians, the Romans, the Mediæval Italians, the Dutch, and, though more sparingly, by the English also. In Italy, Holland, and Flanders the material assumed its most decorative forms; but with regard to ordinary purposes, the clamp-burnt brick, made in the Home Counties, has perhaps never been surpassed. For facings and finer work, there are endless varieties in quality and colour, carefully prepared and burnt in kilns. The introduction of tiers of hoop iron give a tenacity to modern brickwork never previously attained.

Among the recent improvements in the bricklayer's province must be noted the drain-pipe, which, from its superior efficiency, has entirely superseded the old method of construction.

The common tiles made in the neighbourhood of London are by no means equal to those of Staffordshire, rendered, by intense firing, blue in colour, and of a semi-vitrious appearance; but except where more exclusively appropriate, tiles for roofing have been displaced by slates from the Welsh and Irish coasts, and from Westmoreland. A double layer of slates, in the lower part of walls is an excellent expedient to prevent dampness.

A light and durable covering for turret and other roofs of steep inclination, is afforded by the malleable sheet zinc, introduced within the present century. I employed it, about twenty years since, at the London Corn Exchange, and its success there has been complete; but it must always be of sufficient thickness, and so laid as to admit of free expansion and contraction, according to the varying temperature of the atmosphere; and it should never touch another metal, the galvanic action thus set up being a most destructive agent.

Gutters ought, in domestic and substantial buildings, to be always lined with the best milled lead, in pieces of moderate size, so that the buckling by heat and eventual cracking may be prevented.

With respect to native stone quarries, those of the Isle of Portland seem likely to maintain their wonted supremacy; for the inquiries made in reference to the Palace of Parliament do not seem to have brought forward any permanent rival, and Portland remains the king of freestones. It ought to be always used for external steps and window sills, even where other kinds are, from economy or colour, employed for ashlaring and other dressings; but for interior purposes, we have many very eligible kinds.

The application of cast iron to structural purposes has, to a considerable extent, supplied the place of those wooden girders, which are so conspicuous in old houses, and so commonly the subject of defect; for not only were they frequently too weak in themselves, but threw accumulated strains upon walls at indiscriminate points, and without the slightest additional fortification. The philosophical experiments of Hodgkinson and others demonstrate the properties of this material so clearly, that quantity and power may be kept in the most exact ratio ; but until this recent period, the builder had not less reason than the warrior to keep Butler's couplet in mind,

" Ah me ! what perils do environ
The man that meddles with cold iron ;"

a danger from which, however, he is now more than ever exempted, by the modern conversion of wrought-iron plates into beams of enormous strength.

The vast forests which furnish their annual contributions to the ports of the Baltic, afford the best balk timber for constructive carpentry, and the finest deals for the finishings of the joiner. Much of the imported wainscot comes from the same geographical districts ; but we have also excellent woods, of these and other species, from our wide-spread colonies. It

[will

A HOUSE FOR THE SUBURBS.

GROUND PLAN.

A. —Vestibule.

B.—Hall.

C.—Library.

D.—Drawing Room.

E.—Garden Entrance.

F.—Dining Room.

G.—Staircase.

H.—Water Closet.

I.—Housekeeper's Room.

K.—Storeroom & Back Stairs.

L.—Wine Cellar.

M.—Ale Cellar.

N.—Pantry.

O.—Kitchen.

P.—Scullery.

1.—Larder.
2.—Dairy.
3.—Coals.
4.—Knives.
5.—Laundry.
6.—Wash-house.
7.—Furnace Room.
8.—Conservatory.
9.—Dust.
10.—Water Closet.
11—Shed.
12.—Gardener's Tool House.
13.—Piggeries.
14.—Cowhouse.
15.—Roots.
16.—Coals.
17.—Scullery.
18.—Stairs.
19.—Living Room.
20.—Corn and Chaff.
21.—Stable.
22.—Harness Room.
23.—Coach-house.
24.—Hay and Straw.
25.—Poultry.
26.—Dung.
27.—Pasture.
28.—Kitchen Garden.
29.—Flower Garden.
30.—Terrace.
31.—Drying Ground.
32.—Farm Yard.

A HOUSE FOR THE SUBURBS.

LAN OF THE PRINCIPAL OR GROUND STORY.

T. MORRIS, ARCHITECT.

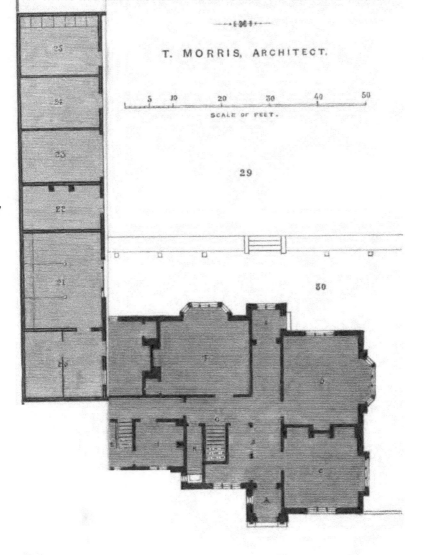

SCALE OF FEET.

27

will, however, be convenient to touch upon
the subject of materials, in discussing the plans
to which the reader's attention is now invited.

So fastidious are some writers on the
aspects of rooms, that one may " box the
compass" round and round without pleasing
them; but, like the poet's truthful flower,
we will seek the sun's morning smile upon
our bed chambers, and from the " embow-
ered windows" watch his evening rays with
the eye of affection.

The drive, then let us premise, is on the
North East, toward which is placed the broad
glazed oak door of the vestibule. The outer
steps and the threshold are of Portland
stone; but now what do we tread upon?
A tesselated floor, more indestructible than
stone, more beautiful than mosaic, tasteful
and rich in geometrical devices, and a very
triumph of colour. No wonder, when the

talents of Owen Jones and Digby Wyatt
have been devoted to the advancement of
this department of industry, and such makers
as Minton and Hollins of Stoke, and Maw
of Benthall, throw their enterprising liberality
into its prosecution.

Proceeding into the hall, we are pleased
with the "storied pane" of the mullioned
window, an embellishment of great effective-
ness; and as the quantity required is seldom
large, it need not involve a serious outlay.

Among the kinds of ornamental glass
suited to the windows of modern houses there
are, *First*,—The "enamelled," where a pattern
is produced by laying a coat of vitrifiable
material over the entire surface and brushing
out the device through a stencil plate, before
fixing the ground by burning in the kiln.
When two coatings of enamel are used it is
termed " enamelled and flocked," and as both

sides of the glass are here laid with semi-opaque
grounds, the intricacy of the design may be
much increased.

Second,—" Embossed," where the effect is
produced by coating the glass with a ground
capable of resisting fluoric acid. This ground
is removed where the pattern occurs and the
acid then eats away the surface of the glass,
leaving the pattern indented, after which it is
thrown into silvery relief by grinding the
original surface of the plate.

Third,—When instead of the stencil plates
the devices are produced by " hand etching,"
there is no limit to the intricacy of the device,
and the art of ornamenting glass becomes
closely allied to that of engraving on copper.
Sheets of ruby, blue, yellow, purple, green,
and other colours may be used instead of plain
glass, and treated by any of the foregoing pro-
cesses, but these are all of modern origin and

differ essentially from the mosaic or leaded system employed in our ancient churches and halls, they are, however, economical substitutes, and it has been suggested to me that leaded figure work without colour might at little cost be appropriately introduced for staircase and similar windows with great pictorial effect.

This idea perfectly agrees with my own observation, that great interest is sometimes excited by windows painted in a low subdued tone, where richness of design and a varied degree of opacity are more relied upon than vivid colour, and supports a previously formed intention for the fenestral treatment of a church recently entrusted to me for completion.

The impetus given to glass painting has raised the modern school to a high yet still ascending rank, and among the examples in domestic edifices few perhaps exceed in size or elaborate device the staircase window of twenty-one lights at Beau Manor Park, where the liberal hand of Mr. Perry-Herrick, the heraldic accuracy of Mr. J. G. Nichols, and the art of Mr. Warrington, combined to lend historic interest and deck with tints of sparkling harmony the crowning work of my late leader here and friend.

In winter, the comfort of the whole house depends on the hall stove, an object to which corresponding ingenuity has been devoted; but those only are worthy adoption which instead of merely raising the temperature, provide for the constant influx of warmed air.

The first of the family rooms is the library (a name derived from the *librarii*, or literary slaves of the ancients). It has been the scene of wondrous changes, although in this country, down to the invention of typography, a small

muniment room was sufficient for the largest
lay residence. Its style should be unpretend-
ing, yet not mean, the bookcases and their
contents proclaiming its immediate destination. The chimney piece, of some hard stone
or marble, may be appropriately surmounted
by armorials. Mr. Gandy, the architect of
Exeter Hall and the beautiful chapel in North
Audley Street, once occupied my present chambers, and finding in them a chimney piece of
his design, choice in material, but insignificant
in size, I took some pains to preserve the relic
of so great an artist, and made additions in
the same taste. The grate has no visible iron
work, except the moulded frame and the fire
bars, the back part being of fire lumps, and
the front of dark enamelled slate. The whole
seems well suited to the suburban library.

The drawing room being the chief apartment for evening use, is that to which embel-
lishments, both permanent and portable, are

most liberally devoted. The floor is carefully prepared, the boards very narrow, the nails concealed, and perhaps a veneering is laid, to secure a smooth and finished surface; but if beyond this an inlaying of damask parquet be intended, care must be exercised, in order that the crossing of the grain may not also cross the lively *voltigeurs.* The windows, whether of that most graceful form of illumination, the bow, or not, are certainly glazed with highly polished glass, imparting brilliancy to every object seen through it. The ceiling is enriched with elegant devices, in plaster or composition, relieved with delicate and cheerful tinting, heightened by some fanciful *morceaux* of the painter's art, and harmonised by judicious, rather than prolific gilding. The walls invite the hand of the decorator, though operators of this class usually require more *chastening* than a son from the most loving of fathers. Looking glasses should always have something to reflect; and although sometimes the endless repetitions of opposite mirrors cannot be commanded, the position of the chimney and the *étalage* should always be studied with reference to this rule. The chimney piece is usually of pure statuary marble, with more or less of sculptural enrichment; and the grate exhibits the highest finish in lustrous steel, German silver, *or molu*, or porcelain.

In mansions large enough to have several rooms of the same or closely analogous kinds, a *suite* affords convenience as well as grandeur; but in houses of a moderate scale it is, in many respects, preferable that each room should be quite distinct from the rest; and it is very requisite to have a garden entrance, instead of making a window serve also the purpose of a door, so that apology must be unnecessary for having extended the corridor up to the porch, next the terrace, as will have been noticed in coming to the dining room. This has a character quite distinct from the others, and ought to be rich and stately, though somewhat grave.

Before lath and plaster had superseded wainscoting for the sides of rooms, every panel admitted some device, and the multiplicity of parts alone helped the impression of finish. A late excellent friend, although a composite of the architect and builder, who did a suburban house for himself on the way to Harrow, introduced in a dado the bearings of all his customers, or those who had helped him on in the world; and a son of Esculapius was advised the other day to fill the panels of his ceiling with the hatchments of those he had helped out of it. A bay window is very grateful here; for " they be pretty retiring places for conference, and, besides, they keep both the wind and the sun off; for that which would strike almost through the room, doth scarce pass the window."

M

The chimney piece should be massive (and among native materials few are more appropriate than the splendid serpentine of Cornwall), the grate inclining to the quaint and heavy.

In the management of ceilings, where lightness does not happen to be desired, there is great danger of falling into the opposite of clumsiness, and thus of destroying the effect of loftiness; but the difficulty of the question came upon me a short time since, in the fullest force, when a client protested against the adoption of artifice to increase the apparent height of his rooms. " They are 12 feet high," said he, " and they shall be made to look 12 feet high, neither more nor less."

The use of Turkey carpets renders a bold margin of parquetry very suitable in the floor of this room.

PLAN OF THE CHAMBER STORY.

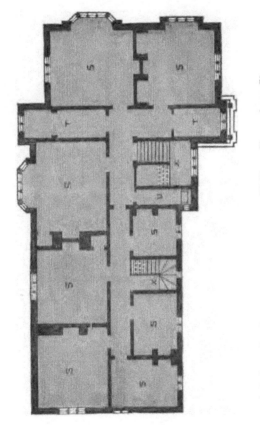

S.S.S.—Bedrooms.   T.T.—Dressing Rooms.

U.—Water Closet.   X.X.—Stairs.

It may be assumed that the joiner's work in the drawing room will be *flatted* in party colours, with or without a relief of gold, or be grained, in imitation of satin wood or bird's-eye maple, and the other parts "like the "unwedgable and gnarled oak." The hinges, whether of brass or iron, plain or ornamented, whether without shifting plates to hide the screws, and whether "rising" or not, should be of the best quality; and the locks should be such as, combining the essential advantage of modern inventions, act with the ease and sweetness which result from simplicity and good workmanship, yet afford the security due to strength and ingenious contrivance.

Ascending the stairs, which are of Portland, or, it may be, fine Painswick, stone—for, as they are always carpeted, the latter is very admissible—we come to the chamber floor, upon which are arranged eight bed rooms (if none be subtracted for nursery or bath room), and there are two dressing rooms.

A water-closet adjoins the staircase on this as on the principal floor; and a word or two may be said here on the internal plumbing of the house.

In places where no other means of supply exists, a well must, of course, be sunk, and a force-pump set up; but in the environs of London that expense may generally be saved, although I think the "Companies" obnoxious to very just reproach in respect to deficient supply through which, under the present system of internal closets, gases of the foulest and most poisonous character, fraught with fevers, cholera, diphtheria, and death, are admitted into our dwellings while the cause is perhaps unsuspected.

I have found it advantageous in practice

PLAN

OF

THE MEZZANINE STORY.

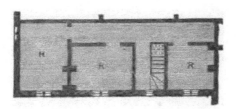

R. R. R.—Bedrooms.

to take the soil pipe quite up to the gutter, letting it serve also to carry off the rain water, and when that cannot be done to lead a small pipe up through the roof, so that the foul air instead of rushing at every opportunity into the house may find a ready exit at the top.

I used to visit a family, who resided in an old house at Islington. The smell from the drains was intolerable to strangers, though not noticed by the inmates, all of whom had, however, most indifferent health, and the doctor was seldom absent. I built a house for them afterwards, at a short distance from town, and their health has improved in so marked a degree, that medicine is almost unheard of. Now the foul air from the drains escapes unchecked or nearly so the moment the closet is without water!

Iron pipes are taking the place of lead to a considerable extent, and are sometimes furnished with a coating of enamel, which seems to render their sanative nature complete. A large cistern should be fixed in some part of the roof, and, when so protected from frost, slate may be safely employed. It is very desirable that cold water, at least, should be obtainable on the upper floor of a house; and, by proper arrangements, hot water may be also provided for at a slight additional cost.

The house would be very incomplete without a bath, but whether on the upper or *mezzanine* story, shall be left to the reader's choice, as we descend the back stairs to look into the three rooms there located, any one of which would be large enough for the purpose; and there are so many methods of fitting up, that the prevailing wish, whether of economy or completeness, may be exactly met; but to make the kitchen fire available, it is necessary to come to an early decision.

Continuing to descend, we are again on
the ground floor and among the " offices," the
first being the housekeeper's room, with its connected store closet, both replete with presses,
shelves, drawers, and such like receptacles.

The wine cellar has its arched brick bins
for bottled nectar, and space besides for the
cask, branded with mysterious signs of crowns,
diamonds, grapes, Vs, Os, and Ss, proclaiming
its contents to be so very very old, and super
superior.   There is a good lock on the door,
with   a   bright little key, which " master"
always keeps with the jealousy of a Blue-
beard; but the next cellar holds that which
everybody in the country drinks with so
much satisfaction—the bright, the generous
" October."   Let others

> " Chronicle small beer."

Adjoining this is the cubiculum, in which
Mr. Buttons performs the several departments
of his vocation.

We now approach the precincts of the *cordon bleu ;* and as we have a distaste for the *plain*, and are afraid of the *professed*, trust to meet with a *thorough good* cook! and so will endeavour to surround her with every needful appliance.

The kitchen floor has been, to some extent, prepared for by the layer of concrete spread over the whole area of the house: upon this there may be a course of hollow bricks, and then a finish of freestone, or some neat and cheerful pattern in tiles.

We will confide in our *Cuisinière*'s house-wifery with the fuel, and indulge her predilection for an open fire; a strong six-feet range, with wrought-iron bars. The oven at the side shall be large, and constructed with a double casing of wrought iron, allowing the fire to act on all its surfaces except the front, and giving the visible top suffi-

[cient

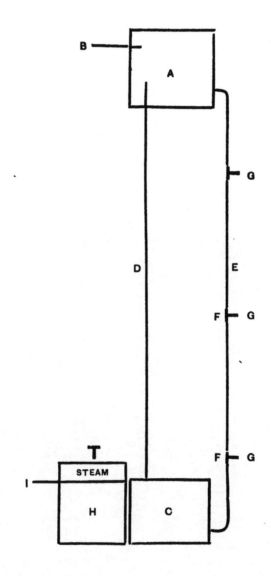

HOT-WATER APPARATUS,

IN CONNEXION WITH THE KITCHEN FIRE.

——•——

A.—Upper Boiler, or hot cistern.

B.—The pipe by which it is fed with cold water.

C.—Boiler at the back of kitchen range.

D.—Ascending pipe from lower to upper boiler.

E.—Descending pipe from upper to lower boiler.

F.F.F.—Junctions, or **T** pieces, with pipes G.G.G. for hot water service to the various floors, &c.

H.—Boiler kept filled by the cold supply pipe I. to the proper level, but not full. The steam is formed in the upper part, and from the **T** piece at the top it may be conducted by pipes in any direction.

cient heat to keep vessels upon it at a boiling temperature. Then the said oven has its shelves, revolving trivets, regulating ventilators, and dampers, so that it may be susceptible of exact management, be quite closed up for *soaking*, or admit the steam to escape when *browning* is the object.

The massive table seems fixed to the soil, like the great beds of our forefathers ;—then the dresser, with its drawers, subjacent potboard, and surmounting shelves, testify our care ; even to that wicked little cupboard, into which " Missus" herself dare not pry, although "Cook" is presumed to have no " perquisites."

We intend to have a supply of hot water throughout the house, and a few steam kettles, necessitating something like the arrangement in the preceding sketch ; and the range shall further have its spit-racks,—as, although a single movement and dangle will suffice, the smoke-jack cannot willingly be dispensed with, and the iron ring in the chimney has not been forgotten.

The scullery has not been stinted in dimensions, for manifold are the offices it subserves. A smaller range qualifies it as an occasional kitchen. If a pump be needed, its best place is here, by the sink, which is wisely lined with thick lead, and whose indentations bear witness to the breakages its yielding nature has prevented. The copper—not made of iron, as some quibbling contractors have now the hardihood to pretend that a copper can be—and the brick oven, for bread, take up further portions of the space, which might, at first, have seemed too great.

The coal oven consists of a very flat arched chamber of brickwork, and the door is in the middle of one end. On one side of the door is a furnace, like that of an

N

ordinary copper, where the fire is lighted and continues to burn while the oven is in use. On the other side of the door is the smoke flue; and the oven is made hot by the rapid passage of the flames and smoke from the furnace to this flue, just inside the central door. It may be kept at the requisite heat throughout the day, and batch may follow batch uninterruptedly, so that its advantages over ovens of the old construction must be at once apparent.

A covered way leads us to the larder, with its dresser and shelves of slate, and ventilating gauze of galvanised wire.

Adjoining to this is the dairy, also fitted with slate dresser and fly-guards to the win-· dows. The floors of both may be laid with hard Broseley tiles, and the sides lined with the finer and thinner sorts proper for the purpose. In a dairy just completed was a large central bench or table, consisting of a thick slate top, on arched brick supports. In the middle of the table rose a jet of water, for securing coolness in hot weather; and the waste fell into a sunk trough, formed at the edges, and so into the drain.

It would be negligent to pass unnoticed the new churning apparatus, which acts with wonderful rapidity; and being furnished with an outer casing, may, by means of hot or cold water, be regulated to a suitable temperature in any season.

We pass the coal-house to reach the laundry, in some convenient part of which must be a drying closet, with its half-dozen horses —*running horses* they may be called, as they run backwards and forwards with their alternate charges of wet and dry clothing. The closet is heated by the dry heat of the ironing stove, and secures a rapid desiccation in all weathers; and on the large table is just now placed the portable spring mangle, which produces the effect of a heavy roller, though when not in use takes up no room.

The wash-house is by no means unworthy attention, either in construction or fitting up. The floor is strongly paved, and dryness provided for; while a free escape for the unavoidably humid atmosphere is secured without injurious draughts. An ample supply of pure soft water has been also—and at whatsoever cost—obtained; and the troughs have both hot and cold supplies. The detergent power of steam, and the simple and inexpensive means by which it can be generated and applied—a close boiler only, without machinery of any kind—strongly recommend its introduction; or there is the French portable laundry, sold by Mr. Kent, in Holborn; and the small, but most efficacious, wringing machine must not be forgotten.

SECTION OF A FILTERING TANK.

Yet with all the improvements which render the *Blanchisseuse* independent of the weather, the drying ground, with its posts and lines, may be properly retained, together with a shed, for preserving the posts and other matters relating to these offices generally. We conclude our visit to the kitchen court by peeping into the dust-house, which we see has the clever rotatory sifter, which supplies the smokeless fuel for the hot plate we ought to have noted in the kitchen.

THE SOFT WATER TANK.

The tank I have devised for the reception and purification of soft water is formed by sinking a well in the earth and constructing the bottom and upright "steening" with brick in cement, so as to render the inside perfectly watertight, the top being finished with a dome and "man-hole," as it is called, in the usual way.

A ring of two or three courses of bricks
without mortar is built in the middle, and
upon this brick support a cylinder of earthenware, open at the lower but closed at the upper
end, is fixed.   The suction pipe of the pump
is passed into this cylinder, which is then surrounded by coarse rubble succeeded by a layer
of closer ballast, A.   Then a stratum of charcoal, B, covered by a bed of sand, C, upon
which some tiles are loosely laid.

The pipe from the pump draws the water
from the vessel at the bottom of the tank, and
is supplied by a subsiding action in the fluid,
by which as it passes through the filter bed it
is perfectly freed from impurities.

The rain-water from the roofs of the buildings may be conducted by pipe drains, dis-
charging their contents into the tank near the
bottom of the dome, as shewn in the annexed

section, and an ample quantity of clean soft water be ever at command.

At the end of the offices more particularly called domestic, and terminating the range by which the flower garden is flanked, is placed the conservatory, which cannot be dismissed without a few words, of much greater utility, I fain would hope, than a mere form of enumeration; for instead of any rational attempt being usually made to economise solar heat, and retain by such uncostly means an equable temperature, a perfect *frigidarium* is usually first set up—all the sides and all the roof of glass—and then a wasteful expenditure of fuel and attention is imposed to correct so thoughtless a proceeding.

Loudon has shewn that every square foot of glass cools a cubic foot and a quarter of enclosed atmosphere per minute—as many

degrees as the inner temperature exceeds
that of the outer air; so that, assuming the
heat inside to be 66°, and outside 44°, every
100 superficial feet of glazing would depress
125 cubic feet of air 22° every minute, and
the largest body of atmosphere would thus
be rapidly reduced to the external level,
but for the warmth artificially generated
within.

The plea upon which the better and more
substantial principle of construction observed
in the plant-houses of the last century has
been departed from, seems to be that of
obtaining more light, and it has been facilitated by the low price of glass; but it is,
in fact, a groundless argument, for light is
so extremely diffusive, that, as illustrated in
the Pantheon, at Rome, a single foot of glass
will illuminate, in an agreeable manner, 3,000
cubic feet of space.

Attention to this property has led to great improvement in the lighting of picture galleries, shewing that a moderate proportion of glass suffices to remove shadow from every part of an interior at all appropriate for pictures or for plants.

It should be understood by all gardeners, that the atmosphere being the vehicle of frost it rarely penetrates the soil more than a few feet, and the mean temperature of the earth increases with the depth attained. A well and deep boring in the chalk for instance, are the source of supply for the new company at Plumstead, and the water, when first raised has a constant temperature of fifty-two degrees of Fahrenheit. The earth may therefore be regarded as a reservoir of heat, and the value of sunk pits is well known in horticulture; but the principle upon which that value is based has not been extensively applied. A trough formed in the ground and covered with a ridge of glass, the two sloping sides meeting at top like the letter ∧ has been found suitable for grape vines; and Sir Joseph Paxton has recently patented a folding portable roof of a similar form, to be set on earthern banks or slopes, dispensing with all other glass except at the ends,—thus, I am happy to find, that while my hobby of a solar greenhouse has its distinctive characteristics, the general economy of heat is receiving attention in other quarters.

With this fact before us, we may safely have walls on the North and East sides; and if the roof be also of opaque materials, to act as a reflector on those quarters, and transparent only on the South and West, the heat acquired during the day will be sufficient to exclude frost in the night, except in seasons of intense cold, and the contemptible flimsiness of appearance, now so general in these structures, will be obviated.

Where a love of floriculture exists, the conservatory will be the source of much enjoyment, and must be treated with becoming care. Many methods for opening the windows have been tried; but nothing is really better than double-hung sashes, to open from top and bottom, because they are easily regulated, the wind has no effect upon them, and the plants are not interfered with. The floor cannot be more suitably formed than with encaustic tiles, and the sides may be lined with them, the wire and trellis, for climbing plants, being duly provided.

Although it appears a first duty to save the heat afforded by Nature, it is still necessary to secure a source ever at command, and under exact regulation. These ends seem most satisfactorily effected by the circulation of hot water, in iron pipes, the dark and rough surfaces of which are favourable to radiation, or throwing off the heat they contain.

Atmospheric air is capable of holding, in imperceptible suspension, a considerable amount of moisture. The maximum is termed the Dew point, and the charge increases with the heat of the air.

To prevent rapid evaporation is one of the gardener's anxieties, and he therefore places troughs, containing water, in connexion with the heated pipes, to supply the moisture absorbed by the air, and prevent coldness about the roots of the plants. The water applied by the syringe is also temperated to the appropriate extent; but I think a thermal fountain would be at once the most effective and the most elegant method of combining warmth and moisture. As the syringe requires some force in its use, it may be as well to substitute for it a hose-pipe and spreader, fed from one of the raised cisterns.

The advantages derivable from " orchard

houses " have been rendered so apparent of late
that we may expect to see them very generally
adopted in gardens of all sizes. They may be
constructed of rude inexpensive materials, and
a temperature, like that of Southern France,
obtained without fire heat.

The house of the groom and gardener is
the first noticeable object on entering the
farm or stable yard, not inconsiderately
huddled up behind sheds, but open and
healthful. It is as Loudon has properly
suggested, his castle for the time being, and
its inmates are neither constrained to remain
in-doors or forced into contact with their
superiors. It has one neat living room, a
kitchen fitted with a cooking range of modern
contrivance and a copper. Adjoining to this
is the coal house : up stairs there are two
airy bed rooms, and the eight-day turret clock
so necessary in an insulated establishment, is
over part of the staircase.

Then we come to the cellar for roots, which are of such high importance in an establishment of this kind.

The cow house adjoins and is proportioned for three cows and a calf pen; and the range on that side concludes with the piggeries, divided to separate the store hogs from the fatting exemplification of

" Daily more a swine he grew."

On the opposite side we find the poultry house, duly fitted with nests and perches, and if a dovecote be desired, it may be contrived in connection with this part, and the aerie will surmount the roof. Though often made an upper loft, the barn for hay and straw will be most convenient on the ground.

The coach house is spacious enough for a close carriage and a " Newport Pagnel," and has its neatly battened folding doors hung to

wood posts, with the strong and easy working
ball and socket hinges. If there be a jet of
warm air from the harness room, it will be
advantageous in cold damp weather.

The harness room is lined all round with
narrow deal boarding, and abundantly supplied
with brackets for saddles, collars, harness, and
bridles, girths, stirrups, reins, and traces
enabling the groom to make that display of
care and system in which he so worthily
delights. The fire is open, as its radiant
heat is very much required in drying, and
there is a tolerably large boiler attached to
the grate, in order that hot water may be
always obtained.

For several of the places last described,
including the women's court, or drying ground,
where the usage is not rough or the traffic
great, the floor may be of asphalte. I have
recently employed it at the houses near the

o

Adelphi Theatre, to be occupied by the Corps of Commissionaires, a body, I may notice, formed under the patronage of H.R.H. The Commander-in-Chief, "who knows how genuine glory is put on," ably seconded by Captain Edward Walter, and the *débris* of warfare is thus raised to a position of utility and independence, by their patriotic exertions.

The stable yard would be better if laid with some sort of stone pitching, and the syenite from Lord Stamford's Groby quarries would be excellent if obtainable at a moderate cost in the London market. A pump or water trough is here indispensable.

The stable deserves our best attention, but the chief danger at the present moment is that of running into unserviceable detail. The floor ought to have just so much inclination as is requisite for dryness without

rendering it irksome to the horses. The old
Dutch clinkers were very hard and indestructible, but these qualities are now attained
in home manufactures. The Staffordshire
chamfered bricks are very hard and afford a
secure footing. Paving bricks of the stock
kind, and the club bricks, when well burnt,
are also very suitable.

The old method of draining by strong bell
traps and double gratings, fed by stone or
brick channels, has not been worthily
replaced by the slight surface gutters and
covers lately brought forward.

No stable can be commended which is
without a chambered roof, or in other words
a roof and ceiling, as forming the most
efficient safeguard against the rapid change of
temperature.

With regard to the material of stable

fittings, it ought to be born in mind that its heat and humidity render it very favourable to the growth of fungus, and if wood be employed containing the least tendency to decay, it is soon destroyed, and on that account the walls ought to be dry before wood work is introduced. Cast iron has been commonly used for many years in the heel posts, ramps, and sills of stall divisions, as well as for racks and mangers; but where close economy is not looked for, bold turned posts of oak with thick iron rings, oak sills on brick foundations, and double battening capped with oak and surmounted with an open railing, so that the occupants of neighbouring stalls can see each other, make the most appropriate divisions and best withstand the intercourse with hoofs of steel.

For the same reason it is better to batten all the sides for about five feet, and line the upper part with glazed wall tiles. In some

stables lately erected in Leicestershire, where
slate is obtainable, the mangers and some
other parts were made of that material in
preference to wood or iron, and with very
satisfactory effect.

Rooms for chaff and corn are attached.

Chaff and corn! Corn and chaff! Lie
down my pen, I'll write no more. No, for
thou hast given to " criticizing elves" their
cue ; and " though reasons were plentiful as
blackberries," mine will surely be rated like
the voluble Gratiano's, but " as two grains of
wheat, hid in two bushels of chaff." Dry,
husky thought, no more of thee.

It would indeed, I seriously fear, be quite
intolerable to pursue these notes into the
questions of fences, earthwork, and planting,
although they strictly appertain to the subject, and may in practice receive attention

from those to whom my best acknowledgments are due—the Readers of " A House for the Suburbs."

NOTE.—The manner in which the honest struggling poor, are thrust and elbowed from place to place, each more unworthy and pernicious, is admittedly disgraceful; and therefore, the idea of conveying labouring people, to and from villages especially adapted to their occupation seems at first attractive; although the least reflection shews, that it cannot be applicable to any class, inferior to the skilled artificer, whose working day does not exceed a dozen hours. But there are vast numbers dependent on their daily industry, whose employment is so precarious, so extended and variable in time and place; and so meagre in its reward, as to make the very mention of country habitations, mere false, delusive mockery; and the disingenuous source from whence such dreams proceed deserves to be unveiled.

The all-pervading love of money, dictates the driving out of those, who when employment fails, becomes at once suppliants to the hardest of all Boards, the cold, unsympathising guardians of the poor;—yet, until it can be shewn, that landholders do not enclose entire parishes within their domains, and so free themselves from rates, how can we give pre-eminence in sordid policy, to the Corporation of London, when it dislodges the meaner citizens to make way for grand thoroughfares, and wholesale rate-payers? The vote of City money, towards the erection in *Westminster*, of houses to receive the poor cast out of *London*, is nevertheless an example of *liberality* that excites admiration!

Railways, and improvements of various kinds, must however continue to absorb space in the most valuable parts of the Metropolis, houses must be destroyed to make room for public works, the poor, augmented in numbers, must be compressed within narrower and rapidly contracting limits; and the inverted and antagonistic principle now in action continue the work of transition. Some remedy must needs be sought, some antidote discovered!

In my very humble opinion, the relief is not distant. Rents, obtainable from properly devised, and well constructed houses, will be found to repay the capitalist. Cupidity will be defeated, by the generalization of poor rates; and large areas will be supplied by the gradual removal of Prisons, Union Houses, and Lunatic Asylums, to situations more appropriate to their respective purposes, than the midst of a great commercial capital. What humanizing changes are thus in store, it would seem visionary to predict; but the suggestive seed, now planted, may haply be developed by the agencies of a progress, divine in its appointment, and immutable in its direction.